SINGLE WOMEN/
FAMILY TIES

NEW PERSPECTIVES ON FAMILY

NCFR Published in cooperation with the National Council on Family Relations

Series Editor: **Maximiliane Szinovacz**
Old Dominion University
Series Editor-Elect: **Linda Thompson**
University of Wisconsin, Madison

Books appearing in New Perspectives on Family are either single- or multiple-authored volumes or concisely edited books of original articles on focused topics within the broad field of marriage and family. Books can be reports of significant research, innovations in methodology, treatises on family theory, or syntheses of current knowledge in a subfield of the discipline. Each volume meets the highest academic standards and makes a substantial contribution to our knowledge of marriage and family.

SINGLES: Myths and Realities, *Leonard Cargan and Matthew Melko*

THE CHILDBEARING DECISION: Fertility Attitudes and Behavior,
Greer Litton Fox, ed.

AT HOME AND AT WORK: The Family's Allocation of Labor,
Michael Geerken and Walter R. Gove

PREVENTION IN FAMILY SERVICES: Approaches to Family Wellness,
David R. Mace, ed.

WORKING WIVES/WORKING HUSBANDS, *Joseph H. Pleck*

THE WARMTH DIMENSION: Foundations of Parental Acceptance-Rejection Theory,
Ronald P. Rohner

FAMILIES AND SOCIAL NETWORKS, *Robert M. Milardo, ed.*

FAMILIES AND ECONOMIC DISTRESS: Coping Strategies and Social Policy,
Patricia Voydanoff and Linda C. Majka, eds.

SINGLE WOMEN/FAMILY TIES: Life Histories of Older Women,
Katherine R. Allen

Other volumes currently available from Sage and sponsored by NCFR:

THE SOCIAL WORLD OF OLD WOMEN: Management of Self-Identity,
Sarah H. Matthews

ASSESSING MARRIAGE: New Behavioral Approaches,
Erik E. Filsinger and Robert A. Lewis, eds.

THE VIOLENT HOME, Updated Edition, *Richard J. Gelles*

SEX AND PREGNANCY IN ADOLESCENCE, *Melvin Zelnik, John F.
Kantner, and Kathleen Ford*

SINGLE WOMEN/ FAMILY TIES

Life Histories of Older Women

KATHERINE R. ALLEN

**Published in cooperation with
the National Council on Family Relations**

SAGE PUBLICATIONS
The Publishers of Professional Social Science
Newbury Park   London   New Delhi

For information address:

SAGE Publications, Inc.
2111 West Hillcrest Drive
Newbury Park, California 91320

SAGE Publications Ltd.
28 Banner Street
London EC1Y 8QE
England

SAGE Publications India Pvt. Ltd.
M-32 Market
Greater Kailash I
New Delhi 110 048 India

Printed in the United States of America

Library of Congress Cataloging-in-Publication Data

Allen, Katherine R.
  Single women/family ties: life histories of older women /
by Katherine R. Allen.
      p.   cm. — (New perspectives on family)
  Bibliography: p.
  ISBN 0-8039-2804-1. — ISBN 0-8039-2805-X (pbk.)
  1. Single women—United States—Family relationships—Case studies. 2. Widows—United States—Family relationships—Case studies. 3. Aged women—United States—Family relationships—Case studies. 4. Working class women—United States—Family relationships—Case studies. 5. Life cycle, Human—United States—Social aspects—Case studies. 6. Life change events—United States—Case studies. I. Title. II. Series.
HQ800.2.A45   1989
305.48′9652—dc20
                                                                    89-6383
                                                                    CIP

FIRST PRINTING 1989

Contents

Series Editor's Foreword

White middle-class couples and nuclear families have served and continue to serve as the major target group of family research. All too often this emphasis on specific population groups produces more than results of limited generalizability: The attitudes and behaviors revealed in such research take on a normative character; they become standards of comparison. Among the best examples of this standard-setting quality are, perhaps, early conceptualizations of the family life cycle, conceptualizations based primarily on the life experiences of the white middle class. Increased awareness of racial and ethnic minorities and the growth of some "alternative" life styles have led to heavy criticisms and reformulations of the original family life cycle stages. Yet, some of the standards inherent in earlier investigations linger—some life styles, even when widely practiced (premarital sexuality, divorce) continue to be seen as different, alternative or problematic.

In her volume, Katherine Allen explores life experiences among one of the most stereotyped population groups, never-married women. Based on a life course perspective, the work investigates central themes in the lives of never-married women born at the beginning of this century. Variations in the lives of these women are documented through accounts of the respondents and contrasted with the life experiences of widows. The results are striking not for their differences but for the many similarities in life themes—the centrality of family relations, the importance of children.

Research such as this is needed to question and correct our many preconceived notions of "normal" family life (whatever that may be) and to acknowledge that it is its potential for diversity and adaptation which made the family one of society's focal and lasting institutions. Allen's work provides us with important insights into the variations and similarities in the life experiences of never- and ever-married women. We learn much about the meaning of family obligations in women's lives and about the life of working-class families at the beginning of this century. But even if Allen's volume did little more than further the demise of standard white middle-class notions of family life, it would constitute a valuable contribution to the literature, a contribution fully deserving of sponsorship by the National Council on Family Relations.

—*Maximiliane Szinovacz*

Acknowledgments

This book has been many years in the making. The lives of the women revealed here and the process of discovery that accompanies life history research are so compelling to me that I have found it difficult to let go. My son, Matthew, was born during this process and learned to walk and talk as I crept through the writing and revisions. Fortunately, many people have helped me along the way, and I would like to thank them for helping me finish this book.

I am grateful for the guidance of my professors and friends at Syracuse University. Robert Pickett helped to shape many of the ideas in this book. Thank you for sharing your knowledge with me, for reading so many drafts of my work, and for continuing to be my mentor and friend. Christine Riley has been a constant source of support and intellectual challenge. Our walks around Syracuse are etched in my memory, and our ongoing friendship continues to sustain me. I am grateful, as well, for the contributions of Professors Harlan London, Ruth Wynn, and George Bodine. Barry Glassner was especially important in providing advice about the research process. The Syracuse University Senate Research Committee funded the data collection. The Metropolitan Commission on Aging in Syracuse gave me permission to conduct my research through the Senior Clubs and Centers Council.

I am also grateful to colleagues and friends who read portions of this work, offered suggestions, challenged my thinking, and supported the completion of this project. Alexis Walker read the entire manuscript. For her friendship and intellectual vigor, I am most grateful. She has taught me a great deal about caregiving and collaboration, and this book is informed by her careful scholarship. Joyce Williams read several versions of the initial chapters. I value her wise insights about taking a broader perspective. Many thanks to Alan Booth, Jane Gilgun, Norval Glenn, Norah Keating, Ralph LaRossa, Suzanne Steinmetz, and Linda Thompson, all of whom have read various portions of my work and contributed to the ideas contained in this book. My colleagues Jennie Barr and Lillian Chenoweth make the day-to-day challenges of academic life a pleasure. Thank you for your love and support. Conversations with

Judith Cannon, Roberta Ezell, Mary MacGregor, and T.J. Stone have informed my ideas about women's lives. Thank you for caring so much. For earlier contributions, I thank Sylvia Groopman, Robert Ryder, and Judith Waugh.

Maximiliane Szinovacz was an excellent editor. Her guiding hand and high standards provided the push for a more encompassing perspective. Thank you, Maxi, for making such an important contribution to this work. The two anonymous reviewers, whose insights guided the revision process, were especially appreciated. I wish I could tell you in person how much you contributed to the book.

To my parents, Jack and Betty Allen, and my brothers, John, Dan, and Doug, and my sister, Beth, thank you all for your encouragement. Beth, you have always been my inspiration. To my husband, Kenneth Special I dedicate this book to you. Thank you, Ken, for your love and commitment and for helping me keep all of this in perspective.

Finally, to the generous and remarkable women who shared their lives with me, I am most grateful. It is your story I have set out to tell. I hope this book is careful with your lives.

—*Katherine R. Allen*

1

Introduction

OVERVIEW OF THE STUDY

Women are socialized to structure their life course decisions around an orderly sequence of marital and parental roles (Bernard, 1972; Chodorow & Contratto, 1982; Elder & Rockwell, 1976). Normative events in the family life course of a married mother include marriage, birth of first child, first child starts school, first child graduates from high school, first child marries, first grandchild born, 25th wedding anniversary, husband retires, husband dies, first great-grandchild born. Most of these events are tied to biological processes (Rossi, 1980) and reflect transitions in one's family of procreation. They are socially recognized "rites of passage" (Van Gennep, 1960), ritualized in ceremony and celebration. Children's lives are marked by birthdays, graduation, and confirmation. Married women are honored with a wedding and anniversaries. Mothers are celebrated on Mother's Day. Romance, marriage, and motherhood are sentimentalized on Valentine's Day. But, who gives cards to maiden aunts? There are no rites of passage for never-married women.

The exclusion of never-married, childless women from the family life course emphasizes their deviance in relation to married mothers. A variant approach, on the other hand, suggests that there are other events and processes that distinguish the family lives of lifelong single women. A life course approach to permanent singlehood is informed by historical and contemporary trends and allows a woman's affiliation to her family of orientation to be viewed within the individual, familial, societal, and historical context. This approach compares the cultural norm of compulsory marriage and the alternative strategy of lifelong singlehood.

The present study led to a discovery of certain female life course patterns that elaborate the family-keeping activities of single women. Qualitative in-depth interviews were conducted with 30 women from the 1910 birth cohort to discover aspects of their life histories that contributed to their work in the family. Initially, 104 women were interviewed; then a matched sample of 15 never-married women and 15 widows were interviewed further. The unmarried women remained single their entire lives and did not bear children. The widows followed the traditional life cycle pattern of marriage, motherhood, grandmotherhood, and widowhood (Duvall, 1971; Glick, 1977; Hill & Rodgers, 1964).

A life course perspective guided the study by tracing one cohort's history over time (Elder, 1977; Hareven, 1978, 1982a; Uhlenberg, 1988). The qualitative research design allowed the women to express their views with minimal interference from the investigator. The retrospective in-depth interviews allowed events, processes, and patterns in the women's lives to emerge. The themes reported here link the theory and method used to guide the study as well as the substantive findings about working-class women's family history. The themes include the enduring cohort effects of hardship in childhood and young adulthood, the interdependent careers of women and their kin, and the ongoing interplay over the life course between family and work careers. An enduring, auxiliary family role for the single women was discovered. This role was essential to maintaining the family of orientation, and it augmented the important work of women who reproduce and extend the family. The juxtaposition of two marital groups from the same birth cohort allowed the meaning of singlehood in the later years, when the never-marrieds and the widows shared a single status, to emerge. These themes reveal the contributions of a cohort of lifelong single women to the sustenance and continuance of their families.

Most of the women in this study were the children of immigrants. They were from working-class homes and lived in working-class neighborhoods at the time of the study. They were raised with a familistic ideology (Hareven, 1977; Laslett, 1972) and experience of living, working, and struggling together. This familistic ideology, a holdover from feudal times, retains some of its strength in working-class families, probably more so than in middle-class families (Rapp, 1982; Smith & Valenze, 1988). An individualistic ideology, on the other hand, promoted by the liberal moral theory of the 18th century Enlightenment and used to justify the industrialization and urbanization of Western societies, has allowed more autonomy for middle-class families (Smith & Valenze, 1988; Treas, 1977). Working-class family life, on the fringe of a capitalist system, has always been more precarious (Scott & Tilly, 1975; Smith & Valenze, 1988). State intervention and welfare programs, rather than individualism, have probably reduced the strength of the familistic ideology in the working class (Boris & Bardaglio, 1987; Zaretsky, 1982).

It is primarily women who bear the responsibility for sustaining families, especially in the working class (Rubin, 1983). Women pool resources to prevent family disintegration during times of insecurity, and they rely on a vast network of kin relations to do so (Hareven, 1987; Komarovsky, 1962; Rapp, 1982; Rubin, 1976). Using the analogy of a safety net, Rapp (1982) explains women's role as the bridge between ideology and reality, that is, between how meager a household's resources really are versus how independent a family's position is supposed to be. It is women who "must constantly test, strain, and repair the fibers of their kinship networks" (Rapp, 1982, p. 175).

Marriage strategies, another alternative that families use for survival, are rooted in the class structure of a society (Bourdieu, 1976; Hareven, 1984; Watkins, 1984). Remaining unmarried and attached to the family of orientation was an expectation for some members of the 1910 cohort (Allen & Pickett, 1987). The never-married daughter, who retained a primary connection to her family, followed an alternative strategy to marrying and producing her own family. The unmarried daughter's family-keeping role was promoted by the family under certain circumstances, such as when a parent was widowed and other siblings had left home. The role of family keeper was a legitimate but covert strategy that some families used to maintain their cohesiveness.

THE LIFE COURSE PERSPECTIVE

The experiences of a cohort of never-married and widowed working-class women are considered in this study from a life course perspective, which is an interdisciplinary approach to individual and family development. This perspective builds on the original formulation of the developmental approach to the family (Hill & Rodgers, 1964), but moves the issue of family development away from a consideration of normative stages toward a consideration of individual and family variations across the life span (Chudacoff & Hareven, 1979; Elder, 1977; Hareven, 1987). Compared to other theoretical frameworks in family studies, the developmental approach is unique in its sensitivity to time (Rodgers, 1973). The developmental framework views families as long-lived groups with a history and allows for a broad range of applications, from family interaction to family-society transactions (Rodgers, 1973). A life course approach has been used recently to discover the complexity of family life in the past through studies that are sensitive to how time, context, and process structure individual and family experiences (Elder, 1981).

Influential life cycle studies include the pairing of family developmental theory with various research designs. Glick (1977) offered a demographic analysis of women's life cycle changes over time, where developmental theory was used to interpret changes in women's reproduction, mortality, and marital histories. Hill's (1970) classic study of three generational families and their consumership patterns employed retrospective history taking and a longitudinal design. Spanier, Lewis, and Cole (1975) addressed the conflicting results in previous studies of marital adjustment and satisfaction over the family life cycle, where evidence has been found for linear declines and curvilinear patterns. They analyzed data from three coordinated studies and found only partial support for curvilinearity. Their analysis highlights some of the problems in operationalizing the family life cycle by using cross-sectional designs, since it is not often feasible to study families longitudinally. They suggest other explanations for curvilinearity, such as cohort effects, age effects, social desirability response sets, and cognitive consistency theory.

Other critics of the developmental approach claim that the stages merely reflect changes in marital and parental status (Elder, 1977). The use of a priori stages in the developmental view provides only static snapshots of household membership (Berkner, 1973; Hareven, 1987; Trost, 1977). The family life cycle concept and its broader theoretical framework are more useful conceptually than empirically (Nock, 1979). Spanier et al. (1975) note that the approach has yielded rich descriptive studies of family life over time, but its explanatory power has not been realized. Also, the original life cycle model of establishment, expansion, contraction, and dissolution through death was based on an ideal-type, or normative family, that probably never existed (Mattessich & Hill, 1987).

Hill and Mattessich (1979) emphasize the flexibility of the family developmental approach in responding to criticism of its theoretical and empirical limits. For example, Aldous (1978) extended the theory to elaborate on the sibling relationship into old age. Hill (1986) proposed a life cycle stage model of the single parent family career. In addressing these changes, Mattessich and Hill (1987) suggest that although revisions of the particular contexts of family development are possible, the original character of family development as unfolding through hierarchical and universal stages remains an important assumption.

The present study builds on the theoretical strengths of the developmental approach (i.e., its earlier linkage to time, the interdependence of individuals and families, and the relationship between families and other institutions), but departs from the idea of a normative family life cycle. By substituting the concept of life course variation, permanent singlehood and the auxiliary family keeping roles of single women in old age are viewed as structurally essential features of working-class family life for women born in 1910. Singlehood was a survival strategy that was selected by some women or chosen for them by their family. It was not deviant from the norm of marriage; rather, it was one of many pathways that women could follow.

Temporal Distinctions

The emphasis on time in the developmental and life course perspectives reflects a consideration of the interdependence of the individual, the family, and society throughout history. Chronological time, measured in linear units such as the moment, day or year, is unidirectional; time and age become meaningful only within a particular social-historical context (Elder, 1974; Erikson, 1975; Mills, 1959).

Historical time is a second temporal distinction. People born at the same time are members of a cohort. All cohorts make fresh contact with unique historical and social heritages which color their perceptions of the world. They are "entitled to participate in only one slice of life—their unique location in the stream of history" (Ryder, 1965, p. 844). Economic depressions, wars, scientific discoveries, social reform movements and the like have different meanings to people depending upon the age at which they experienced them. Members of the same birth cohort share this background as they age (Hill & Mattessich, 1979). The social-historical context structures life course opportunities, leaving individuals varying degrees of freedom to make their own choices. For women in this study, the social-historical context in which their lives unfolded spans the 20th century. Yet, 19th century values are evident in their choices due to their socialization by elders born in the 1800s (Smith, 1979). This context includes those of working-class and immigrant status.

Family time refers to changes over the family life course that come with the intersection of individual and family biography and transactions between the family, economy, and state (Elder, 1977). Family time is similar to the idea of the family life cycle, but without the assumption of universal, sequential stages. Family development is a continual process, and the stage concept merely freezes it in order to analyze family dynamics and change (Hill & Rodgers, 1964). Chudacoff's (1980) comparison of the two approaches suggests the departure from the stage concept in the life course perspective, which "is less concerned with the fact that most individuals experience a stage of parenthood than it is with when in an individual's life parenthood begins and ends" (p. 275). Feldman and Feldman (1975) replace the concept of stage with "subcareer," defined as separate but overlapping modules or event histories in the individual and family life course. Career is a more dynamic concept of change, attuned to variations that occur due to the timing, sequencing, and spacing of life events as individuals move in and out of different family roles and statuses.

Individual time is the individual life course, that is, the inevitable and irreversible process of birth, maturation, and death (Hareven, 1982a). Elder (1977) defines the life course as "the pathways individuals follow through age-differentiated roles and events" (p. 282). Lives are structured by separate but interrelated careers such as the marital, parental, occupational, and residential. Each career is composed of a series of events, roles, and changes which are defined by a particular timetable and sequence. Transitions refer to turning points that signal one is entering a new phase of life or exiting from an old one. All phases of life are interrelated, and the present must be examined in relation to the past (Elder, 1977).

Through these temporal distinctions, the family can be viewed as a unit of individuals whose personal careers are mutually contingent. The emphasis on careers and transitions, when they occur or whether they occur at all, seems more realistic and flexible than the assumption of stages. Rather than focus on the normative character of a developmental cycle, a life course perspective focuses on variations that result from multiple career lines. In the present study, five life course careers are considered: family, friendship, health, residential, and work.

Interdependence and the Process of Change

The concepts of dependence, independence, and interdependence can be used to interpret life course decisions. Dependence is a structural feature of working-class life, in the relationship of the family, economy, and state (Rapp, 1982; Scott & Tilly, 1975). Dependence is played out in individual lives as well. In this study, it was expressed in the ways women put their family's needs ahead of their own and was related to life cycle events such as the death of a parent or the birth of a child. In the later years, dependence coincided with the physical decline of aging, when visual problems, for example, required some women to sell their home and move to an apartment complex for the elderly. Thus, dependence was associated with a loss of selfhood, through a conscious sacrifice or a loss of control.

Independence, on the other hand, was a process of gaining selfhood, of individuating. The women viewed independence as finally getting a break from their family. Becoming independent was described either in behavioral terms as an event or role change, or in psychic terms as an inner transformation where a woman felt she had become different. For example, the death of a spouse or a parent in later life gave some women their first independent feeling of "this is my life now."

Finally, women are interdependent with their families to varying degrees over the life course within this structure of cooperative and competitive individual and family needs. Their interdependence links the family of orientation and the family of procreation within a broader context of household, family, kin, and class structure. Never-married women in this study retained their membership in the family of orientation, but they were also connected to ancestors, lateral kin, and younger kin. The widows held a primary allegiance to the family of procreation, but they also were connected to kin.

The nature of women's family connections over the life course is shown in how women maintain and extend their families through the processes associated with interdependence. Although interdependence can be measured in discrete life course events, it occurs over time. The process of change is revealed in transitions of independence from and dependence on the family. For these women, change occurred when decisions were made between conflicting needs or demands, as in a choice between marrying and supporting an aging mother. This study of women's life course development does not measure change as progressing through a series of stages, but instead, examines the timing of the changes, how the women perceived and defined the changes, and the significance of the changes for themselves and their families.

Integrating the experiences of never-married women broadens the meaning of family as a mutual relationship between the individual and her kin. Differences between traditional and never-married women exist, but not necessarily in stereotypic ways. This holistic framework of mutuality is consistent with women's historic connection to caring activities and institutions (Finch & Groves, 1983; Gilligan, 1982; Smith & Valenze, 1988; Walker, Pratt, Shin, & Jones, 1989). The analysis is sensitive to the contextual factors of time, place, and class that structure the nature of women's life course decisions for self and family (Rapp, 1982; Watkins, 1984). Comparing never-married women to their traditional peers demonstrates that their life course development is rooted firmly in these multiple contexts.

PREVIEW OF THE BOOK

Retrospective interview data, a life course perspective, and working-class women's history were combined to illuminate the contribution to family development of lifelong single women in relation to their widowed peers. The ideas that guided this study are described in Chapter Two, and the research process is discussed in Chapter Three. Chapter Four examines the social-historical context of the women's childhood, revealing their background of familistic values that drove home their sense of family obligation. Their early experiences of dependence upon relatives and state institutions led to enduring cohort effects by structuring their expectations that life was hard. Chapter Five focuses on the experiences of the never-married women and widows as young adults and the processes leading to singlehood, delayed marriage, and early marriage. Chapter Six examines mid-life variations in their experiences of family keeping and caregiving. Never-married women cared for parents, widows were involved in their marital careers, and both groups cared for children. Women's historic connection to the home is reexamined by contrasting the experiences of widows with their never-married peers. Chapter Seven examines the meaning of singlehood in old age for each group. The assumption that marital status structures women's lives into categories of never-married or formerly married is reassessed. Chapter Eight examines the family life course careers of women in this cohort. The processes of independence, dependence, and interdependence are suggested as the ways in which women extend and maintain their families over time.

2

Working-Class Single Women in Historical Perspective

PERMANENT SINGLEHOOD IN HISTORICAL CONTEXT

Lifelong singlehood has been a significant alternative to marriage throughout history. In previous centuries and in other cultures, a significant minority of women remained single depending on a complex interweave of economic, social, political, demographic, and historical factors (Chambers-Schiller, 1984; Dixon, 1978; Hufton, 1984; Watkins, 1984). Definitions of singlehood reveal a middle- and upper-class bias and treat it as a unilateral experience, as illustrated by the changing definition of "spinster." Spinster began as a professional term (Hufton, 1984), meaning "female spinner," a task that held some status and was performed by both males and females (Chambers-Schiller, 1984). By the 18th century, spinster became the legal term for unmarried woman and came increasingly to have negative connotations (Chambers-Schiller, 1984, p. 219). Spinster became linked to "old maid," implying "certain pejorative attributes—such as narrowness of spirit and a tendency to gossip over the teacups" (Hufton, 1984, p. 374).

Little is known historically about working-class single women, because "few working-class women have testimony deposited in archives; those who do are immediately suspect in their 'typicality.' Much information about working-class life must come from middle-class pens" (Tentler, 1979, p. 6). Young single girls in 18th century France and England worked as domestic servants, starting out to save money for a dowry. They struggled to survive in a hostile world, often unattached to men or families (Hufton, 1984). Older single women were more likely to join the households of wealthy families as a nurse, nanny, personal maid, or housekeeper (Hufton, 1984). Working-class English women in the 19th century suffered all kinds of indignities and exploitation as domestic servants. Female servants, regardless of age, were always considered "girls," emphasizing their dependent status (Davidoff, 1983). They spent most of their lives maintaining cleanliness in middle-class homes, where "their most important job was to remove dirt and waste: to dust; empty slop pails and chamber pots; peel fruit and vegetables; pluck fowl; sweep and scrub floors, walls and windows; remove ash and cinders; black lead grates; wash clothes and linens" (Davidoff, 1983, p. 44). Hufton (1984) suggests the heroic attributes of the term spinster "to convey the sense of someone who struggled against odds and social disapprobation and yet survived and in some cases made the survival of subsequent generations easier" (p. 374).

Chambers-Schiller (1984) documents the increase of American spinsterhood since the end of the colonial period. The number of spinsters was never more than a few percent in colonial America. By 1780, the percent began to rise and continued through the 19th century: 7.3% for women born between 1835-38, 8.0% for those born between 1845-49, 8.9% for those born between 1855-59, and at the height of the trend, 11% for those born between 1865 and 1875 (Chambers-Schiller, 1984, p. 3). Among 19th century American middle- and upper-class women, spinster became associated with a "cult of single blessedness" and lost some of its association in colonial America with sin (Chambers-Schiller, 1984). Viewed more contemptuously by others than by themselves, the cult of single blessedness was a movement among educated spinsters to bring dignity to their place in society. The legacy of single blessedness fostered an emphasis on marriage or singlehood as a choice for women in the middle and upper classes (Adams, 1976; Watkins, 1984).

Although older definitions of spinsterhood as sinful or disgraceful have given way to contemporary ideas of choice (Chambers-Schilller, 1984, p. 11) or alternative lifestyle (Macklin, 1980), singlehood is still devalued and considered a personal failure. Stereotypes of single women are couched in pathological terms, such as lack of sexual attractiveness or the inability to form an intimate relationship with another person (Adams, 1972), and research has focused on the psychological deficits in single women's personality as compared to the relative health of married women (Adams, 1972; Gove, 1972). However, Stein's (1978) typology of contemporary singlehood as voluntary or involuntary, permanent or temporary moves closer to fulfilling the ideals embodied in singlehood as a choice. Since 1960, singlehood has increased among women born in the 1940s and 1950s (Macklin, 1980; Stein, 1978). There is more appreciation of the heterogeneity among older single women (Braito & Anderson, 1983), and the prevalence of single blessedness has been recognized among successful middle-class women who never married and who are disproportionately represented among professional career women (Carter & Glick, 1976; Havens, 1973). The focus on professional achievement and personal fulfillment, however, obscures the meaning of singlehood for older working-class women. Economic insecurity is a structural feature of working-class family life, and their survival has depended on strong kin loyalty (Hareven, 1987; Tentler, 1979).

EXPLANATIONS OF PERMANENT SINGLEHOOD

Marriage choices are tied to economic, historical, demographic, and cultural conditions. Women are most likely to delay or forego marriage under worsening economic conditions and to choose spinsterhood voluntarily if they have employment opportunities other than marriage (Dixon, 1978). As more women remain single, the social stigma and isolation associated with spinsterhood declines, reinforcing singlehood as a marriage alternative (Chambers-Schiller, 1984; Dixon, 1978). Increasingly, family phenomena are seen as diverse, complex, and variable across individual and group experience (see also Andersen, 1988; Elder, 1981; Hareven, 1987; Huber, 1988; Runyan, 1984; Thorne, 1982). Feminists, in particular, have offered new syntheses of gender and class in relation to women's home and market labor (see also Acker, 1988; Hartmann, 1981; Rapp, 1982; Smith & Valenze, 1988; Tentler, 1979). The incidence of permanent singlehood is a type of family phenomena which defies simple explanation (Dixon, 1978; Watkins, 1984). Examining the correlates of singlehood in a particular culture at a particular time invites a contextual explanation of singlehood for those circumstances. Although Watkins (1984) cautions that such an explanation is still so general that it obscures many particulars of time, place, and class, the use of correlates suggests the varying contexts under which singlehood is tolerated or rejected. Two examples, discussed below, are relevant to female singlehood in early 20th century America.

The Western European Marriage Pattern

Hajnal (1965) identified the historical differences in European and Asian marriage patterns that were distinct until 1940. Since 1960, three patterns have converged toward early and universal marriage (Dixon, 1978). The Western European pattern, characteristic of countries such as Ireland and Sweden, was a high age at marriage and a high proportion of people who never married at all. From 1900 to 1930, Western European women married at 24 or later and at least 10% never married at all. The Eastern European pattern, including countries such as Albania, Yugoslavia, and Bulgaria, was earlier marriage and lower proportions remaining single. The non-European pattern, in countries such as Japan and Korea, was early and universal marriage (Dixon, 1978).

Dixon's (1978) analysis of Ireland, an exaggeration of the Western European marriage pattern, examines economic and demographic pressures that led to the increasing prevalence of singlehood from 1850 to 1950. In 1850, Ireland was typical of northwest Europe. On the average, both sexes married by age 30, and between 10% and 12% remained single. By 1911, however, bachelors constituted 40% and spinsters 28% of individuals aged 40-44. With an agricultural economy, Catholicism, and a stem family structure (Berkner, 1973), permanent singlehood was a legitimate alternative to marriage for siblings other than the son who would inherit the family farm; that is, younger sons and daughters were encouraged to stay at home as unpaid helpers on the farm. Women who did marry no longer worked outside the home, and fertility rates were higher than elsewhere in Western Europe. Marriage was a viable choice only for daughters whose families had saved enough to marry them off into farms as valuable as their own because entire families relied on the slim earnings of one male breadwinner. Otherwise, rural girls saved the dowry themselves as indentured workers or by emigrating to cities or overseas. Under these constraints, marriage was not compulsory for women in Ireland as it was in Asian countries such as Japan (Cornell, 1984; Dixon, 1978) or China (Watkins, 1984).

In societies where most women marry, "remaining single must be justified in terms accepted as legitimate by the community" (Watkins, 1984, p. 313). In Asian societies where parents, elders, or formal matchmakers arrange marriages, singlehood is almost nonexistent (Dixon, 1978). In western societies where individuals find their own mates, they are more likely to delay or avoid marriage. Watkins (1984) extends Dixon's (1978) analysis by noting that the prevalence of singlehood in Western Europe is correlated with the timing of marriage, the sex ratio, economic constraints, and a church that forbade polygyny and elevated celibacy and individual consent. In contrast, dedication to family values and the family's control over arranged marriage and religion led to near universal female marriage in China and Japan. As Watkins (1984) explains, "In Asia, there were virtually no extenuating circumstances that excused remaining single; in Europe and the United States there were many" (p. 313).

Educated American Spinsters Versus Working-Class "Girls"

Another contextual example of spinsterhood contrasts poor single women with middle- and upper-class American spinsters during the 19th and early 20th centuries. Middle- and upper-class American spinsters also followed the Western European marriage pattern noted above (Chambers-Schiller, 1984; Dixon, 1978; Freeman & Klaus, 1984; Watkins, 1984). Chambers-Schiller (1984) studied 100 northeastern, white, native born, Protestant spinsters using books and diaries written by and about these women. Although their education, employment, and literary abilities were unique among women of their era (born in 1780-1840), the themes identified in their writing signaled a new wave of thinking about women's independence. These spinsters articulated "single blessedness" by cultivating the female self and striving for personal autonomy. This ideology departed from the overtly submissive overtones of the "cult of domesticity" among southern women prior to 1860 (Welter, 1966). After the Civil War, the "new spinster" increased, as well, among unmarried women in the South, and by the 1880s, single women were moving west and were able to remain unwed due to the availability of cheap or free land (Chambers-Schiller, 1984).

The status of the 19th century new American spinster in the middle and upper classes was contradictory, however. The maiden aunt's independence from marriage was legitimized by being on-call to her family throughout her life. She was to be devoted to the private sphere and to a life of service to others because "parents, siblings, nieces and nephews, aunts, uncles, and cousins expected a spinster to have no particular occupation and therefore freely sought her companionship, business assistance, nursing, housekeeping, and babysitting services" (Chambers-Schiller, 1984, p. 112). Domestic arrangements for 19th century privileged women, married and single alike, included daily involvement in the emotional life of their family and friendship network (Chambers-Schiller, 1984; Freeman & Klaus, 1984; Smith-Rosenberg, 1975).

Except for marital status, the new American spinster had little in common with poorer single women (Freeman & Klaus, 1984). Working-class women worked for very low wages in factories or domestic service. Private domestic employment was the single largest female occupational category in 1900, replaced in 1914 by factory work (Tentler, 1979). Women from the middle and upper classes "depended upon the large reservoir of unmarried working-class women. Lacking husbands and needing an income, these working-class women cleaned, cooked, served, and made the Victorian and Edwardian middle-class life possible" (Freeman & Klaus, 1984, p. 395). In her study of middle- and upper-class single professional women, Vicinus (1985) reveals how teachers and reformers in England from 1850 to 1920 won their rights and pursued their significant achievements by exploiting class distinctions of morality and the actual labor of lower-class women. Their households, work environments, and female communities (Freeman & Klaus, 1984; Vicinus, 1985) depended on the labor and sexual repression of working-class and poor women on whose behalf, ironically, they advocated reform.

WORKING-CLASS SINGLE WOMEN
IN THIS STUDY

Knowledge of working-class never-married women in the past is like an unfinished patchwork quilt. Evidence about working-class single women in the 20th century is also sparse. A composite review suggests a life of drudgery (Rapp, 1982) and lack of personal fulfillment through education, work, or travel opportunities that are associated with singlehood in the middle and upper classes (Adams, 1976). Unmarried women in the lower classes are more likely to live with parents and siblings, limiting the independence associated with singlehood among wealthier women, and they are still likely to be employed in factory work and domestic service (Adams, 1976; Hareven, 1984).

The present study is consistent with other explanations of singlehood that examine correlates of its occurrence and prevalence (see also Chambers-Schiller, 1984; Dixon, 1978; Hufton, 1984; Vicinus, 1985; Watkins, 1984). However, in this study, the familial context is highlighted by analyzing the life histories of a cohort of working-class never-married women in relation to ever-married mothers. The cohort approach provided the backdrop of changes in family and class life that occurred just before and during their life-time. Their experiences were shaped by the emergence of the welfare state in the 19th century and by its influence on their daily lives. The discovery of their essential role as keepers of the family of orientation, caregivers to parents, and surrogate mothers for descending kin emerged by studying their lives within these contexts.

THE FAMILY LIFE CYCLE OF
WOMEN BORN IN 1910

Glick's (1977) model of the female life cycle provides a general pattern in the lives of women born between 1910-1919. This model, summarized in Table 2.1, combines reproductive and marital transitions in the family life cycle and provides a reference point to compare women in the present study. By using national census data, the model is not sensitive to class distinctions, but the findings do relate to mothers who have been married only once. The approximate period of first marriage for women of the 1910 birth cohort was the 1930s. Their median age at first marriage was 21.4 years, representing a peak in marriage rates from the 1880s to the 1950s, probably because these marriages occurred during the Great Depression. The median age at the birth of the first child was 23.5 and at the birth of the last child was 32. The median age at the marriage of the last child was 53.2 and at the death of one spouse was 63.7.

Table 2.1   Family Life Cycle for Married Mothers in the 1910 Birth Cohort

Event	Approximate Year	Approximate Age
Birth	1910	0
First marriage	1931	21.4
Birth of first child	1933	23.5
Birth of last child	1942	32.0
Marriage of last child	1963	53.2
Death of one spouse	1973	63.7
(Time of interview)	1984	74.0

SOURCE: Glick (1977). Updating the life cycle of the family. *Journal of Marriage and the Family,* *39,* 5-13.
Copyrighted 1977 by the National Council on Family Relations, 1910 West County Road B., Suite 147, St. Paul, Minnesota 55113.
Reprinted by permission.

Thus, women in this cohort spent approximately 8.5 years in the childbearing span, 29.7 years in the childrearing period, and 10.5 years in the empty nest period. Their marital career lasted approximately 42.3 years, and the average number of children born per woman ever married was 2.5.

Glick (1977) estimates that for the 1910 cohort, 93.7% married at least once, and 6.3% never married. Over the 80-year period from the 1880s to the 1950s for which he provides data, there is a curvilinear pattern in percent never marrying, as shown in Table 2.2.

In an analysis of the current elderly, among women 65 and over in 1970, Glick (1979) reported that 36.5% were still married, 3.2% were divorced, 52.2% were widowed, and 8.1% were never married. The slight difference in rates of singlehood between the two analyses reflect differing mortality rates from analyzing women's life cycles over time (Glick, 1977) versus examining the proportions of people surviving to later adulthood (Glick, 1979).

WORKING-CLASS FAMILY LIFE

Families, the Economy, and the State

Among the many ways societies are structured, class, family, and gender are central to the present study. The family and household are products of the economic class structure. In

TABLE 2.2   Percentage of Women Never Married, by Birth Cohort, 1880s to 1950s

	Period of Birth of Woman							
	1880s	1890s	1900s	1910s	1920s	1930s	1940s	1950s
	Approximate Period of First Marriage							
	1900s	1910s	1920s	1930s	1940s	1950s	1960s	1970s
% ever married	91.2	90.9	91.9	93.7	94.6	95.9	94.0	93.0
% never married	8.8	9.1	8.1	6.3	5.4	4.1	6.0	7.0

SOURCE: Glick (1977). Updating the life cycle of the family. *Journal of Marriage and the Family, 39,* 5-13. Copyrighted 1977 by the National Council on Family Relations, 1910 West County Road B, Suite 147, St. Paul, Minnesota 55113.
Reprinted by permission.

Marxist terms, class is the process by which different social relations to the means of production are inherited and reproduced under capitalism. Households are collections of individuals who live together and share resources; the family is the shock absorber to keep households functioning (Rapp, 1982). Because class expresses the material and social relations upon which households rest, women's experience with the family varies systematically by class (see also Acker, 1988; Andersen, 1988; Collins, 1988; Hareven, 1987; Rapp, 1982).

Working-class families in industrial capitalism are dependent upon the hourly wage system for access to resources. Stable working-class households participate in relations of production, reproduction, and consumption by sending out their labor in exchange for wages (Goody, 1972), and it is the work of women to produce, nurture, and send out workers from households (Rapp, 1982). According to feminist revisions of Marxist theory, women's reproductive work and their class relationships form the basis of their oppression and constitute an important part of capitalism (see also Acker, 1988; Andersen, 1988; Jaggar, 1983). Working-class women are multiply disadvantaged by their unequal access to resources and the ways in which their experiences have been constructed by men and middle-class values (Acker, 1988; Thorne, 1982).

Historically, family life and work occurred in the same location, the household, but in the long process of industrialization, the location of reproduction and production became separated (for syntheses of this complex history, see also Acker, 1988; Andersen, 1988;

Hareven, 1977; Rapp, 1982; Zaretsky, 1982). Over the past 150 years, the family wage emerged as the source of exchange replacing old forms of entitlement based in feudalism (Acker, 1988), and with it emerged the ideology of the husband-as-economic-provider (Bernard, 1981b; Hood, 1986). Industrial capitalism created a new relationship of dependency in working-class families. The family wage was distributed from the male wage-earner/husband to the dependent housewife, who kept family life going with her unpaid labor and state benefits to supplement the wage (Acker, 1988). Families are supported by a hidden dimension of women's caring labor in homemaking (Acker, 1988; Bernard, 1981a; Finch & Groves, 1983; Voydanoff, 1988). Primary examples of essential unpaid labor are housework (Oakley, 1985), child care (Ruddick, 1982), and care of the elderly (Brody, 1985; Troll, 1986; Walker, 1983). Women's home labor, i.e., preparing meals, doing laundry, and caring for children, is not affordable if purchased in the labor market (Brown, 1982). Thus, men are dependent on the earnings of their wives and children to supplement the family wage (Hood, 1986; Rapp, 1982). Only during 1940 to 1970 were working-class families able to realize the middle- and upper-class ideal of a male provider and his economically dependent wife (Hood, 1986). Dependence, then, is part of the processes that constitute society as a whole, requiring working-class families to depend on multiple earners and unpaid labor in order to obtain a "living wage" (Acker, 1988).

The welfare state emerged as a resource to help families in the wage economy remain autonomous by offering temporary support to families already strained under industrial capitalism (Boris & Bardaglio, 1987; Katz, 1983; Zaretsky, 1982). Family inadequacy and dependency are predictable consequences in a capitalist system due to occupational risks such as accidents, economic depressions, illness, and desertion by the husband (Acker, 1988). The state administers family "services" when parents and kin are not able, but what began as education and reform has evolved into the institutions and bureaucracies of the welfare state. Since the Progressive Era of 1890 to 1920, poor and working-class families have become increasingly dependent on public charity, whereas middle- and upper-class families, with their greater financial resources, have been able to purchase private services (Boris & Bardaglio, 1987; Rapp, 1982; Zaretsky, 1982). The state helps to create the conditions it is called out to fix, but state supplements are not easily earned nor granted. The struggle to secure state concessions is a long history of social reform, trade union conflict, and political battles. In a wage-based system, if the wage is cut off, the personal relations of distribution are disrupted, destroyed, or altered (Acker, 1988). Destabilization is an ever present threat to working-class families (Rapp, 1982).

There are competing interpretations of the state's relationship to the family. Hartmann (1981) criticizes the welfare state as creating the nuclear family that isolates women in the home and creates their subordinate position in the work force. Lasch (1977) sees the state as usurping the role of the family, but his view does not address the conflict between women and the family. Zaretsky (1982) joins these two arguments by suggesting that the modern family, as a private self-supporting nuclear unit, was created by the state in the liberal and welfare phases of its history. Piven (1985) argues that the state is not as invasive in the lives of poor women as its critics charge, because it has provided alternatives to dependence on men. These interpretations, however, share the perspective that the dependency in working-class families has increasingly extended to state institutions. For women born in 1910, the state was as an ever present reality as they aged, from the orphanages and sanitariums of their youth to the senior citizen housing and social security benefits of their later years.

Kinship and Friendship

Families depend upon their kin network and friends to survive in this system of structural insecurity. By sharing households during relocation, helping each other financially, and caring for aging, sick, or orphaned relatives (Hareven, 1984; Rapp, 1982; Treas, 1977), working-class families pool resources laterally among their kin. In contrast, middle-class families tend to distribute resources lineally between parents, children, and grandchildren in long-term investments such as children's education, setting up private practices, and giving wedding gifts of property (Rapp, 1982).

Friendship is an important part of the network of working-class families. Drawing on Stack's (1974) finding that poor, urban Black families create fictive kin, Rapp (1982) suggests that this process of converting friendship into kinship to equalize resource pooling is also used by working-class families. Middle-class families, on the other hand, convert kinship into friendship to protect themselves from pooling (Rapp, 1982). Friendships are a continuous life course relationship into old age (Bell, 1981; Matthews, 1986; Milardo, 1988). Friendship communities, where women live and work together, have been a structural alternative for spinsters and widows historically, regardless of social class, as Vicinus (1985) found among educated teachers and reformers in late 19th and early 20th century England, and Hufton (1984) found among working-class women in 18th century France.

Working-class social networks are related to relocation and mobility. In the 19th century, kin groups facilitated migration from Europe to North America by operating as a satellite homebase. In Hareven's (1982b) study of the Amoskeag Mills in New Hampshire, relatives were the major brokers between work and family systems by recruiting and placing workers in the factory. In contrast to both 19th century Lancashire (Young & Willmott, 1957) and 20th century East London (Bott, 1971) where the kinship networks of working-class families remained embedded in the industrial town, the geographic distance involved in migrating to America altered this historic pattern (Hareven, 1987). Although the process of immigration and industrialization have dispersed kin to a greater degree in America than in Europe, kinship and friendship networks remain an essential feature of working-class life, as qualitative studies in the mid 20th century have found (Bott, 1971; Komarovsky, 1962; Rubin, 1976). Being able to maintain frequent contact with kin and friends is still an important factor in where working-class families choose to live (Lee, 1987).

Working-Class Marriages

Working-class marriages in industrial societies are characterized by sex role segregation, lack of intimacy and communication, and problems associated with strong kinship bonds (Langman, 1987). Qualitative studies of working-class marriages have found that young women marry early to become independent and escape from an unhappy home (Bott, 1971; Komarovsky, 1962; Rapp, 1982; Rubin, 1976). Yet, many are pregnant within a year or are pregnant when they marry (Rubin, 1976). Economic independence is impossible for most women in a wage-based economy, creating inequality between men and women (Acker, 1988). Middle aged working-class women studied by Acker, Barry, and Esseveld (1981) were realistic about their chances of independence without their husband's income. After venturing into the occupational realm, their concentration in low paying jobs with little room for advancement made them realize how dependent they were on marriage and how fearful they were outside of it. Komarovsky (1962) and Rubin (1976, 1983) also discuss women's pain when they realize that marriage does not live up to their expectations of independence and satisfaction. Yet, seeing marriage as an escape has been an enduring part of the experience of young working-class women. Kessler-Harris' (1977) study of Jewish girls in factories and sweat shops around 1900 showed that the girls planned to marry as soon as they could because they could see no future for themselves except as a married housewife. Nearly a century later, the women in Rubin's (1976) study still reported this ideal of marriage as an escape from drudgery, low pay, and parental control.

Alcoholism, desertion, divorce, and premarital pregnancy are problems affecting all families, but the lack of a financial cushion makes them potentially more destructive in working-class marriages and families (Rapp, 1982; Rubin, 1976). Consistent with national data, 40% of the adults in Rubin's (1976) study had an alcoholic parent, and 50% experienced desertion or divorce in their childhood. Komarovsky (1962) found that lack of intimacy was the common experience in marriage, and for the very few couples who interacted as individuals, rather than according to rigid sex roles, marital solidarity was enhanced. Bott (1971) found that the kinship network, necessary for survival, also undermined the marital relationship by reinforcing sex role distinctions in marriage. Women turned to female relatives, especially their mothers, which reinforced their marital tensions.

Women's Work

By 1875, more women were entering the work force in manufacturing centers and urban areas. They began in domestic service, but as the immigrant population swelled, young unmarried daughters were sent out to work in factories. Jobs tended to be segregated according to gender, age, and ethnicity during the period of Tentler's (1979) study from 1900 to 1930. Italian immigrants dominated flower making in New York; Jewish immigrants dominated the garment shops; Polish immigrants dominated boxmaking. Tentler (1979) reported that from 1875 until the 1930s, the majority of the female labor force consisted of young unmarried daughters, which is consistent with Mason, Vinovskis, and Hareven's (1978) study of female work patterns in Massachusetts in 1880. The familistic values of their native countries prepared them to subordinate their wages, labor, and education to the family's survival and probably contributed to their exploitation, abuse, and segregation at work. Yet, working apart from home gave these immigrant daughters some independence from their families and more control over their own lives (Hareven, 1987; Tentler, 1979).

Once married, women were expected to leave the labor market, but married mothers supplemented their husband's wages by taking in sewing, laundry, and boarders. Homework wages were lower than market wages, and not enough to support a family unless supplemented by the labor of older children (Tentler, 1979). As boarders, nonrelatives became part of the network of resources working-class households used to survive (Modell & Hareven, 1973). Keeping mothers in the home was not realistic for female headed households, which were exceptionally poor. Tentler (1979, p. 165) reported that widowed and divorced women were three times as likely to be employed as married women who lived with their husbands; in 1900, 32.5% were employed; in 1930, 34.4%.

Family and work roles have always been entwined for working-class women, with women employing a flexible entry and exit from jobs in the labor market depending on the needs of their families (Hareven, 1987). Studies focusing on working-class marriages (Komarovsky, 1962; Rubin, 1976) as opposed to working-class women have emphasized the importance of family over work. These studies found that women preferred to stay at home and worked only from economic necessity. Recent research, however, has emphasized the intrinsic rewards working-class women receive. Ferree (1984) argues that the dual career model falsely assumes that only middle-class women work for psychological reasons. Qualitative studies of married working-class women (see also Dabrowski, 1983; Ferree, 1984; Rubin, 1976) present a similar awareness that housework and child care are isolating activities. Labor market work can be rewarding economically, and Dabrowski (1983) found that women derive pleasure, satisfaction, and meaning from their work, even in entry level or monotonous jobs. This is not to deny the structural barriers that continue to keep women in jobs segregated by class, gender, and race (Andersen, 1988), and without more education, a woman is unlikely to get promoted beyond her class level (Dabrowski, 1983). However, recent studies highlight a theme that was evident in the historical literature. Both work and home environments can be oppressive and isolating for working-class women, but not as much as being sequestered exclusively in one without the support of the other.

For middle-class women, the ideology of homemaking and motherhood as the "natural" sphere of adult women has allowed just one exception: "the never-married spinster who is expected to commit herself seriously to being a librarian or a school teacher in lieu of the family" (Lopata & Steinhart, 1971, p. 29). This observation is consistent with findings that older never-married women are highly educated, professional career women (Carter & Glick, 1976; Havens, 1973) and that significant employment in a satisfying occupation is one of the crucial factors in older never-married women's personal and social adjustment (Baker, 1968). Yet, this middle-class bias obscures the experiences of working-class single women. As Keating and Jeffrey (1983) found in their study of never-married and ever-married Canadian women from the 1910 to 1920 birth cohort, without access to the same resources or occupational rewards as professional women, non-professional women do not organize their lives around the worker role, in spite of their lengthy work histories. Working-class women's history reveals the interrelationship of family and market work.

Ethnicity

The patterns noted above are very general; in reality, working-class experience varies with race, ethnicity, geographical mobility, and historical context (see also Mindel & Habenstein, 1976; Rapp, 1982; Ryan, 1973). Race is as important a distinction as class and gender. Minority groups, such as African-Americans, Asian-Americans, Native Americans, and Hispanic Americans, have distinct histories which differ from the majority population and are subordinated socially, politically, and economically. Their differential treatment requires analyses that do not mirror the biases of dominant American culture (Wilkinson, 1987). The history of Black women has been especially obscured by white culture and by studies of Black families, requiring new analyses that are sensitive to class, race, and gender (see also Hull, Scott, & Smith, 1982; Jones, 1985; Stack, 1974; Zinn, Cannon, Higginbotham, & Dill, 1986).

On the other hand, Tentler (1979) found that apart from race, which deserves its own analysis, the experiences of white immigrant American working-class families from 1900 to 1930 shared similarities that allow some generalizations. She found that gender and class were more important than ethnicity in structuring the lives of the immigrant women and families she studied. Her study concentrated on working women's history in the major industrial cities of Boston, New York, Chicago, and Philadelphia, with primarily Irish, Italian, Jewish, and Polish immigrants. They shared the experience of strong family loyalties and being sent out to work to help support their families. Tentler's (1979) findings are consistent with other studies of kin control over work, migration, and individual life course decisions in the late 19th century to the early 20th century among various European immigrants (see also Hareven, 1982b, 1987; McLaughlin, 1971; Scott & Tilly, 1975).

SUMMARY

Little is known about the lives of older single working-class women. From the literature on working-class families in general, it is evident that unmarried women were well connected to their families, particularly among immigrant groups around the turn of the century. Missing from this composite of working-class family life is a more complete understanding of never-married working-class women. Some evidence is accumulating that is sensitive to the contexts of time, place, and class, but the historical literature has a class bias and favors the lives of educated women who wrote diaries or had books written about them. The contemporary literature on working-class families, with its marriage bias, renders the experiences of single women invisible, and the contemporary literature on never-married women focuses only on successful career women. The intention of the study reported here is to add to our understanding of working-class single women by addressing their permanent singlehood within its familial, social, and historical context.

3

The Research Process

SAMPLE SELECTION

The research process began with "insider's knowledge" (Taylor & Bogdan, 1984), an essential feature of the qualitative method. I used my insider's knowledge of the aging services community to structure the data collection and sample selection process, to get started in the field, and to inform the questions asked of the participants. The general questions guiding this study were: How did lifelong single women perceive their lives in relation to widows' lives? How did widows perceive their lives in relation to single women's lives? How did family history and life history intersect over the life course?

Permission to conduct the study was obtained from the Area Agency on Aging, which coordinated 122 senior citizen centers, clubs, and tenant groups. The directors of 38 sites were contacted, and 29 provided participants. It was not possible to obtain a representative sample of never-married women from the 1910 cohort; a compromise was devised to select the sample systematically by obtaining participants from all parts of the metropolitan area. This approach differed from the snowball technique recommended by qualitative researchers (Bertaux & Bertaux-Wiame, 1981; Taylor & Bogdan, 1984) of contacting potential subjects and asking them for names of others in similar circumstances.

Insider's knowledge of the metropolitan area provided an understanding of the social, cultural, and ethnic make-up of the city and county. The inner city was omitted because residents were predominantly Black, and certain wealthy suburban centers were omitted. In keeping with the tradition of others investigating working-class samples (see also Ferree, 1984; Rubin, 1976), the category of neighborhood was used in identifying working-class participants who, for this study, were white, in their seventies, female, and either permanently unmarried or currently widowed.

The directors served as "gatekeepers" (Taylor & Bogdan, 1984) by providing a list of women who were born around 1910 and currently single. The 29 directors provided a total of 193 names, with an average of 6 names from each site (the range was from 2 to 22 names). An initial list of 193 names was compiled; after duplicates were deleted and up to 12 names were selected from each list, a new list was compiled of 139 names from which to begin the telephone screening. Of the 139 women called, 35 women could not be interviewed (28 refused, primarily due to lack of time, and 7 were obviously ineligible). Thus, 104 women agreed to be interviewed, either in their apartment or the senior center.

LIFE HISTORY INTERVIEWS

The mechanics of the data collection process were developed during three pilot interviews. At first, an open-ended interview with six topics was used, but the interview seemed like a quasi-therapy session. In a second pilot, a fully structured interview was used, but this approach led to the reporting of "yes" and "no" answers. By the third pilot, a semi-structured interview guide emerged with open-ended statements and questions to be asked of each participant.

The initial meeting was a face-to-face interview to establish eligibility and rapport. Two documents were completed (see Appendix), the Initial Contact Interview and the Life Events Guide. The first questions on the Initial Contact Interview provided a nonthreatening way to establish rapport. Then, several descriptive questions were asked to establish eligibility. As the women talked about the major events in their lives, the Life Events Guide was completed. Denzin (1978) suggests that completing a life events guide prior to the in-depth interview helps the respondent order her thoughts and decreases the possibility that key topics will be overlooked. The first interview lasted 30 to 60 minutes. If the woman was eligible for the in-depth sample, she was asked to continue with the study for two more meetings.

The second meeting was a semi-structured interview in which the woman was asked to describe the major events in her life. An edited life history interview was used as a compromise between the constraints of interviewing an older person and the assumptions of a qualitative design. Enough structure was needed so that the process was not too frustrating or meaningless for an older person (Job, 1983). Too much structure, on the other hand, would impose the investigator's perspective on the subject (Reichardt & Cook, 1979). Denzin (1978) explains the investigator's editorial role: "For the purposes of theory construction and hypothesis testing, some degree of editing and interspersion of comments by the observer must be present" (p. 218).

An Interview Guide (see Appendix), consisting of open-ended questions and statements, was compiled from the literature review, the research questions, the life course perspective, and the pilot interviews. The interview began with open-ended questions about the woman's current activities, and moved to family relationships, friendships, and details of her background. Then, the Life Events Guide was discussed and her perception of her life as normative or atypical. Several questions were asked to explore how she perceived or measured time in her life. The interview concluded with open-ended statements intended as a summary of her life and the interview experience itself. At the end of the interview, time was taken to discuss her feelings about reviewing her life history. The conversation turned to her home, crafts, pets, and the like. A third meeting was arranged to complete the life history. The tape-recorded interview averaged 90 minutes, and the time spent in the second interview averaged 2 to 3 hours.

Each woman's life history was completed during a third home interview, and forms were developed to obtain comparative data over the residential, occupational, and health careers. The woman was asked for descriptive information about her mother, father, grandparents, uncles, aunts, siblings and their families, and other important kin. Widows were asked for life history information about their husbands and descendants. This process required at least one hour. The women participated actively, either from memory or by looking up dates in the family Bible or an address book. For women who did not remember dates, an attempt was made to ground the event historically, such as "during the Depression."

After the life history data were gathered, a winding down process occurred. The women continued to discuss events and people important to them. The experience of being interviewed triggered many emotions, and reactions were not uniform. Some women had other appointments and were eager for me to leave after the interview. Other women asked me to share a meal with them, as if the process of life review required a ceremony to mark the event. Others requested that I return for a social visit, to take a walk, go to dinner, or see their photo album again. Many women gave me handcrafts they had made. Much time was spent at the close of the final interview to insure that the experience was a positive one (LaRossa, Bennett, & Gelles, 1981). Within a few days of the final interview, a letter was sent expressing the importance of the woman's contribution to the study, including my address and phone number, and offering a summary of the study. Many women responded to the letter by calling to extend an invitation to lunch or to discuss an event or anecdote that had been triggered by the interviews. Finally, a follow-up telephone call or letter was sent to the directors of the senior centers.

THE DATA

Participation in the full study was limited to white, working-class, native-born women from the 1910 birth cohort who followed two distinct pathways. The theoretical models of Glick (1977) and Uhlenberg (1974), derived from their analyses of aggregate data on female life cycle experience, were used as the framework for sample selection. These parameters established the basis for comparison between the two groups in this intracohort study. The first life course included women who remained unmarried and childless during their lives. The second life course included women who married only once, became mothers, and were now widowed. To insure that the traditional female life course was represented among the widowed group, parental status was restricted to women who had at least one child survive through the childrearing process to age 18, which is the census designation for dependency. To limit the effects of bereavement, only those widows whose husbands had died at least one year prior to the interviews were included.

Working-class status was determined by neighborhood, occupation, and education. Income was not used as a criterion because of the difficulty in obtaining this information from older subjects. Respect for their privacy and the desire not to alienate potential subjects were considerations in this decision (O'Rand, 1982). The occupation of women who were self-supporting for most of their adult years was used to determine social class. For the 2 women who were not self-supporting, the occupation of the person who supported them (a husband and a father) was used, a strategy consistent with other studies of working-class women (Dabrowski, 1983; Ferree, 1984).

Of the 104 women who were interviewed initially, only 30 fit the requirements of the in-depth sample. The intensive interviews were conducted with these 30 women, and the data analysis was restricted to their life histories. The sampling procedures insured that only I screened the potential subjects. The attempt to locate single, childless, white, working-class, native-born women from the 1910 birth cohort who did not have college degrees was the major factor in extending the screening interviews to 104 women.[1]

Current demographic characteristics of the 30 women in the study are reported in Table 3.1 and Table 3.2. The women were born between 1907 and 1914; 1910 was the median year of birth. At the time of the study, all the women lived on a fixed income and most received a rent subsidy. They had all worked outside the home, with the exception of one never-married woman and one widow. Currently, the women were retired, with the exception of 3 widows who worked less than 16 hours a week. Ten women completed up to 11 years of schooling, 10 graduated from high school, and 10 received vocational training after high school.

THE SETTING

The women in this study were members of senior citizen centers, sites which provided the context for the initial contact. These groups share characteristics that were evident during my visits to the various sites where participants were located. In addition to government subsidized meal sites, tenant associations and clubs in rural areas offered community suppers. Nearly all sites provided activities such as card games, bingo, craft workshops, and sightseeing tours. In larger centers, men played pool and women participated in activities such as aerobics and Christmas bazaar workshops. Specialized activities such as senior choirs were available at

TABLE 3.1   Educational Background of the Sample

EDUCATION	Completed 7 to 11 years	High School Graduate	Post HS Training	Total
Widows	4	7	4	15
Never-married women	6	3	6	15
Total	10	10	10	30

TABLE 3.2   Primary Occupation

PRIMARY OCCUPATION*	Widows	Never-Married Women	Total
Secretary/clerical	5	6	11
Beautician	1	1	2
Domestic/maintenance	4	2	6
LPN	1	2	3
Teacher	1	1	2
Factory	2	2	4
Homemaker	1	1	2
Total	15	15	30

* Ten widows said they had also been homemakers at various phases in their lives, but only one never-married woman indicated her occupation was homemaker.

smaller sites. Ceremony was important at rural centers. The Pledge of Allegiance and "the blessing" were said before meals, and a patriotic song such as "God Bless America" was sung. At city nutrition sites, community spirit was less evident. People were clustered in small groups with the focus on eating rather than socializing. Many tasks at community functions were sex-typed. Women set and cleared tables, and men carried heavy trays and poured drinks. At city meal sites, workers or volunteers provided these services.

The women also shared a similar home environment. Most of the women lived alone in subsidized housing for the elderly. Their homes and apartments contained collections of furniture and artifacts from 70 years of life, and perhaps from times before that, since many were repositories for family treasures. Typically, homes were neat, comfortable, and modestly furnished. Table 3.3 provides a summary of their living arrangements.

TABLE 3.3 Current Living Arrangements of the Sample

| | *Widows* | *Never-Married Women* | | |
	Living Alone	*Living Alone*	*With Kin*	*Total*
Subsidized Apartment	9	9	2	20
Nonsubsidized Home or apartment	6	2	2	10
Total	15	11	4	30

DATA ANALYSIS

Data analysis began after the interviews and life history forms were completed. All the information collected during the three meetings with each woman was treated as data: Initial Contact Interview, Life Events Guide, verbatim transcript from the tape-recorded in-depth interview, and life history forms. Procedures for coding and analyzing qualitative data were adapted from several sources (Bertaux, 1981; Bogdan & Biklen, 1982; Glaser & Strauss, 1967; LaRossa, 1977; Schatzman & Strauss, 1973; Spradley, 1979; Taylor & Bogdan, 1984). The process of coding involved many thorough examinations of the data in the search for themes and preliminary coding categories. A list was made for each subject, and lists were compared across subjects to determine the themes that were evident in the entire sample. At first, 100 preliminary coding categories were listed, and these were applied to the data in another thorough reading. Codes were found to overlap, so coding families were compiled and tested on the data again. This process was conducted through five examinations of the data, until 52 distinct codes emerged (see Appendix for codes). The data were again reviewed and coded, using procedures described by Bogdan and Biklen (1982, p. 166).

Data analysis was guided by the life course perspective, the research questions, and the life histories of the women as described in their own words. Life history analysis was used in the search for themes and patterns in the data: what was the overall experience for women in the sample; in what ways did the experiences of never-married and widowed women differ; and in what ways were individuals unique? Runyan (1984) explains these three levels of generality in life history research: the search for universals in human experience (what is true of all people); group differences due to sex, race, class, culture, historical period, etc., (what is true of groups); and individual characteristics (what is true of particular individuals).

The themes where the most substantiation was found were incorporated in the final analysis. Substantiation of a theme was guided by the theoretical framework outlined in Chapter One, the historically significant role of unmarried adult daughter outlined in Chapter Two, and the frequency with which experiences and patterns appeared in the descriptive data generated by the life history interviews. Representative quotations from the interviews were used to illustrate the themes that emerged. The purpose of the analysis was to describe the experiences of a cohort of lifelong single women in relation to their ever-married peers. An attempt to explain the discovery of their family subcareers, hidden in existing theories and data about the female life course, was based on the use of correlates of singlehood that emerge for particular groups at particular times (Watkins, 1984).

SUMMARY

In summary, in-depth interviews were utilized to collect life history data on 30 women in their eighth decade. The method was useful in working with an older sample. The open-ended questions facilitated a relaxed and affirmative atmosphere. Respondents revealed the meaning of their life events at their own pace. The methods used for design and analysis guided the study but did not impose pre-ordered categories on the data. The generalizations about women's lives reported here reflect the themes that emerged from careful scrutiny of the data. The chapters that follow reveal how the life course perspective can uncover the interrelationship of individual and family change over time.

NOTE

1. Among the 74 women who were not eligible, 16 were never-married and 58 were ever-married. They were born between 1893 and 1921. Several had college degrees, and 2 never-married women had Masters degrees. The 58 ever-married women var-

ied widely in their marital and parental careers, i.e., married women who were child-less, women who were still married, and women who had been married at least twice. Several widows lost their husbands in the first 5 years of marriage and raised their children in single-parent homes. Also, 18 of the 58 women had been divorced at least once and were living in subsidized housing without the benefit of their former spouse's retirement income.

One factor that distinguished the never-married women from the ever-married women in the group of 74 "ineligibles" was the issue of refusing a second interview. There were 8 never-married women in the larger group who were eligible, yet they did not want to participate further in the interview process. Two women refused because they were too busy to give more than an hour of their time. The remaining 6 refused because they felt "there was nothing left to tell." Their privacy appeared to be very important to them. Perhaps these women were among the socially isolated single elderly described by Braito and Anderson (1983), whereas the women who were eligible and agreed to participate in the in-depth interview process were more active socially.

4

Growing up in Working-Class Families

The women in this study shared a common heritage. The combination of gender, class, cohort, and family experiences located them in similar circumstances. They were raised by people who had been born in the previous century, whose values were shaped by the shared experience of immigration and economic insecurity. The regularities in their lives reflect the cultural milieu in which they were born and reared. Childhood memories contained an awareness that life would be hard, and their recollections revealed their preparation for the harsh realities of working-class life. Those realities included expectations to work hard, the familistic ideology, and firsthand experiences of dependency on kin and welfare institutions.

THE FAMILY INHERITANCE: MARGINALITY AND HARD WORK

Awareness of Ethnic Heritage

At the turn of the century, America was changing from a primarily rural to a primarily urban environment of industrial centers. Urban areas accommodated and grew from the influx of immigrants from southern and eastern Europe. Between 1880 and 1920, these immigrants accounted for one-third of the nation's population growth. They joined the native born American Indian and Black populations as well as the Irish and Chinese immigrants in creating ethnic settlements within the majority culture of urban centers (Abrams, 1973). The ethnic heritage of women in this study is shown in Table 4.1.

TABLE 4.1   Ethnic Heritage of Sample by Marital Status

| | *Birthplace of Parents or Grandparents** | | | | | | |
	Ireland	*Germany*	*Italy*	*Wales*	*Russia*	*USA***	*Total*
Never-married	2	3	3	1	–	6	15
Widow	1	3	3	2	1	5	15
Total	3	6	6	3	1	11	30

*The figures for Ireland, Germany, Italy, Wales, and Russia represent the parents of 6 and the grandparents of 3 never-married women, and the parents of 7 and the grandparents of 3 widows.
**The mixed heritage of the remaining 11 women is some combination of English, Irish, German, Welsh, Scottish, and French Canadian.

One characteristic of people born at this time of immigration was the awareness of ethnic heritage. Nearly all the women in this study identified themselves and others by native background, for example:

I'm German, and I'm stubborn at times.

My father was a big Irishman. He loved to joke with people.

The last wave of immigration to the Syracuse area was Italian, and the parents of 6 women were born in Italy. One daughter of Italian parents revealed her awareness of an immigrant's marginality in relation to other native groups and the dominant culture:

Well, what was wrong with being Italian? They are just as nice as everybody else. Even the Black people. They've got good in Black. . . . We were all brought up in such a different era. We were all just white people. All different races of whites. The Germans didn't like the Italians, and the Irish didn't like the Germans, and they were all fighting among each other. . . . The races were so bad. There was a lot of discriminating then, too. One of my cousins could not get a job because he was an Italian! He changed his name, too, and then he got a job. They wouldn't hire you here in the city if you were an Italian at one time. The Irish were really at the top, then the Germans were next. Then the Italians were at the bottom. Now the Italians are way up, just like the Blacks are starting to get up. It was bad in those days.

Immigration to America often severed kin ties in the native country, temporarily or permanently. To come to America from Italy, for example, one woman's parents left behind their first born child:

> They came over and they never went back . . . they were real poverty stricken. . . . I'm sorry I could never meet my grandparents.

As Tentler (1979) found in her study of working women in 1900-1930, each ethnic group had their own cultural patterns, but they shared the common thread of working-class status. Job security was rare, and the women recalled their parents' difficulties in learning a new language and customs. Fathers typically pioneered the world outside the family, going to night school to learn English once they arrived in America:

> My parents came from the old country, and they were married in Italy and then they came here. My father came first, and he boarded with some people and with his brother. Then they brought over their families after they found a job and got a little money. And then they had their wives come over.

In these young immigrant families, mothers' lives were organized around childbearing and rearing, and they had less access to the outside world than fathers. One woman explained that her parents were married for less than 5 years when her father was killed on a construction site. Otherwise, they would have continued to have a child every year:

> That's how the Italians did it in those days. All my mother's four children were born in the same month, exactly a year apart.

Fathers and Mothers at Work

The fathers of women in the sample were mechanics, masons, factory workers, and carpenters. The women were proud of the contributions of their male kin to building the city and surrounding towns:

> My grandfather was a mason. . . . He built houses and laid chimneys and that sort of thing. . . . He did the cemetery walls down here, where

he would get the stones in the wintertime and crack them on the outside. It's a craft people don't know about today.

When my father came from Italy, he was a mason. He and his two brothers did all that mason work up at the university on the older buildings. The three of them used to walk up there everyday.

Typical of other studies of working-class life, older sons were sent out to work:

My oldest brother had to help support the family. In those days, there was the horse and wagon. . . . I was a little girl then, and I remember my oldest brother getting up early and the milkman would come and pick him up and they would deliver milk. He would peddle papers downtown after school. I don't think they had paperboys then. I think the men purchased their papers for three cents when they came out of work, at the corner.

Once married, traditional values required that women remain in the home to manage domestic and childrearing responsibilities. Consistent with the Western European marriage pattern (Dixon, 1978) and descriptions of married mothers in the working class (see also Lopata & Steinhart, 1971; Mason et al., 1978; Scott & Tilly, 1975; Tentler, 1979), mother's work in this sample was based at home:

In those days, women didn't go out to work. . . . There was nothing, unless you were a teacher or educated in a business career. Very few women worked. If you were married, you didn't work. You stayed home and raised your children.

My father had a good job . . . and my mother never had to go out into the business world. Of course, at that time, ladies, or mothers, didn't go out to work the way they do today. So, we had a very happy home life and a good home. Not too much money, but plenty of money, if you know what I mean.

My mother died when I was 10 years old, so I don't know too much about her . . . she was a good mother. I remember that she was an old-fashioned mother. . . . She used to wear a long apron. She did all of her cooking, and stayed at home raising seven children.

The work histories of these mothers as they aged, however, differed from their daughters' idealization of them as homemakers.

Like Rubin's (1976) 20th century working-class women, a dichotomy was apparent between the ideal and reality. The women in the sample appeared to romanticize the homemaking role of their mothers, but they characterized their own hardship in more realistic terms. They held onto the ideal of a mother in the home, in spite of their personal experience with mothers needing to work to help support the family.

Mothers supplemented the family income by combining market work and homework. Only three non-domestic occupations were held by female kin, all of which were brief—teaching school, working in factories, and selling real estate—but, there were many ways women mixed domestic jobs with homemaking. Periods of family dependency, as in the death, desertion or illness of a spouse, required adult women to use other strategies to support the family. A common strategy was taking in boarders. At any point in time in the late 19th and early 20th centuries, the proportion of urban households that had boarders and lodgers was between 15% and 20%. However, in native born working-class and immigrant households in the industrial north during this time, the proportion with boarders and lodgers approached 45%. By 1930, the Census Bureau reported a decline to 11.4%, and by 1970, to 4.5% (Modell & Hareven, 1973).

Working-class daughters in this study had mixed feelings about their expanded households. One widow's description of living with boarders and kin as a child was consistent with Stack's (1974) and Rapp's (1982) explanations of converting friends into fictive kin:

> My father died in 1925, and we lived with my grandmother who ran a rooming house. We all lived together, my uncles and aunts. . . . It was nice. The roomers there were just like family because they'd been there so long. Then after my father died, he used to do a lot of the repairing on the streetcars, as I said, he died when I was about 15, and then my mother and them still ran the rooming house. But it got to the point where we couldn't run it anymore. It needed repairs and everything, so we sold it for $100 with everything in it, the furniture, the sheets and pillowcases and towels and everything.

In contrast, sharing her home with a widowed mother and a single male boarder was a different experience for a never-married woman, who realized the exploitation of women by men that was part of this extension of the homemaker role. As an adult, she understood her mother's exploitation and was able to change the situation by pressing her siblings to supplement her mother's income:

> My father died in 1942 at age 60; my mother lived to age 88, so there's a lifetime right there, a 28-year period. She was without.... My mother had a pension from my father of $60 a month. He was a Spanish American War veteran. My brothers and sisters each gave, when they remembered to. My mother had a boarder. He paid her $10 a week for room and meals. I finally got rid of that apartment. I had had enough of this boarder business. He was getting away with murder. She did his laundry!

Mothers also took in laundry and did domestic work to supplement the family income, as one widow explained:

> I was the 9th of 10, so my mother was along in years when I can remember. My father was 13 years older and had what they called rheumatism, but what they call arthritis now, so he wasn't able to work, but she worked and took in washing and ironing to keep a home together. And she found time in between to love us.... My father was kind and good, too, but he doesn't stand out like my mother. I only knew a gray-haired father who didn't do things with us.

Another example reveals resource pooling (Rapp, 1982) that occurs through combining child care, market work, and sharing a household. The parents of one widow (who was a newlywed in 1928) divorced, and her mother returned to work:

> My sister was just 5 years old and ready to go to school, and I stayed with her while mother worked. My husband and I lived with her. Then, after I had my baby, I had to stay home. Mother moved into the city and worked in the laundry. We didn't see my father for many years. He just faded, and he never did anything to help my mother support my younger sisters.

Another solution to the death or disability of a father was to send older daughters out to work. One never-married woman from a German background described a family story about her mother as a girl. In 1899, when her mother was a child, her grandfather died and her mother went to work in the hop fields and a knitting mill:

Grandma was all alone, and two of the older girls went to keep house for wealthy families. One of them was a cook in the first old ladies home here, and the other one went to the hop fields. Another one worked in the knitting mill. There were a whole lot of them that were under age. When an inspector would come, all these kids would have to run and hide. He knew that they were there, but he knew also that they had to work. They never really tried to find them very hard. But my mother worked there until she married.

Making do with available resources was a typical experience. Working-class families at the turn of the century were poor (Tentler, 1979), and being resourceful was essential for survival:

> My grandmother gave us some clothes and my mother made clothes, like I remember she made her wedding dress over for me for Christmastime. And I had an aunt that used to bring us girls down quite a few things.

> In those days, men didn't give the wives an allowance. My father never gave my mother an allowance, but she had money because he trusted her. She had worked before she was married and had handled money. But a lot of women couldn't handle money. . . . When I was 17 or 18, I remember a neighbor woman who had a grown-up son and a husband, and you know where she used to get her pocket money? After they went to work, she looked in the cushions in the sofa. She tied it up in a handkerchief and put it in her pocket. That is how the old-fashioned women were.

Although jobs were segregated by gender and age, a characteristic of working-class life in the 19th and early 20th centuries (see also Kessler-Harris, 1982; Scott & Tilly, 1975; Tentler, 1979), mothers and fathers coordinated their work to serve the goal of family survival.

LEARNING THE FACTS OF LIFE

Early Socialization for Hard Work

Family and work responsibilities were learned early in life as girls were prepared to work hard at home and in the labor force in accordance with the survival needs of their family. Being a

daughter in a large family meant more work than the relative freedom granted children in small families. In this study, older daughters were surrogate caregivers for younger siblings, and all girls
helped their mothers with domestic work. The experience of girls in
large families was similar, as 2 widows and 1 never-married woman,
respectively, reveal in the following quotations:

> I was doing everything. I was helping my mother in the house, with
> the laundry, and I did all the ironing. Like 35 and 40 shirts every
> week, and this was without an ironing board, on the table. . . . You had
> to iron everything. There was no such thing as polyester, it was all cot-
> ton. . . . Years ago we used to iron underwear. And blouses had to be
> ironed, and men's pants. . . . I don't iron the way I used to.

> I used to help my mother do the ironing. And I always ironed my
> brother's white shirts. I learned how to iron white shirts at a very
> early age. I learned how to sew on my mother's machine at a very
> early age, and I made a lot of mistakes, but that's the way I
> learned. I knew how to sew before I went to high school when I fi-
> nally took homemaking.

> I was expected to help in the physical part of the housework. When
> there's six kids, and you're the oldest girl, you darn well better, even
> with a big stick, you're going to do the cleaning, help with the wash
> and with the ironing. In those days, there was a big basket of ironing to
> do every week.

Other Facts of Life

Another important aspect of childhood socialization
concerned the ways in which the women were not prepared to han-
dle their own biology, sexuality, and physical disability. There was
an aura of mystery and secrecy regarding female sexuality, and this
was related to lack of education about biology and health. Their
training in these facts of life consisted mostly of misinformation. As
one widow stated:

> My mother and sex weren't related.

Contraceptive information and advice were not available to
women at the turn of the century (Gordon, 1982). Successive childbearing and the physical toll of hard work were correlated with the

high mortality rates of working-class women (Hareven, 1977). Twelve women came from families with 7 to 11 children. Each of them described the toll that motherhood took on their own mother's physical and mental health. One widow's mother left the family after bearing 11 children:

> After she had her seventh child, she had been told by her doctor that she should not have any more children, but in those days, no one knew what the pill was, no one knew how to prevent a pregnancy, and so people just kept on having children, and it was just getting to be too much for my mother, and I would think that at her stage in her life at that time, she needed to get away. And so she would be with her friends once in a while. . . . We have never talked about it. She just left. She would stay away 1 or 2 nights, or a week, and then it got to be all the time. She was just gone. . . . When my last brother was born, and I graduated from grammar school, it was just about the time that she started to go, and she just wanted out, I suppose. I am only guessing because we never talked about it, and in those days we didn't understand.

She discussed the lack of explanation about her mother's multiple pregnancies and her sister's hysterectomy:

> We didn't know what pregnant was. We didn't know that she was going to have a baby the next day, and we'd go to bed at night and we'd wake up the next morning and they'd say, "you've got a new brother; you've got a new sister." I remember one time in particular my mother was taken ill, probably ready to go into labor. My grandmother came to be the midwife, and we asked what was wrong with Mama, and she just said, "She probably just ate some new potatoes and it made her sick." It was an old fashioned idea that if you ate new potatoes maybe they wouldn't agree with you. But she was in the bed, going into labor, and we didn't know.

> My sister had a very tragic thing happen to her when she was dating a boy and was taken sick with what they thought was appendicitis first, and then it wasn't. They thought she had—they called it diseased ovaries—and they removed both of her ovaries so she was never able to have children. . . . When she came home to recuperate, she wasn't getting better. She was still having pain, and they found out it was appendicitis after all and there was never anything wrong with the ovaries.

Two never-married women described how they learned about sex and childbirth, revealing how they had been kept in the dark:

> When I left the orphanage . . . I was a greenhorn, and I even thought the doctors brought the babies and that is how you got them. . . . See, I didn't know any different . . . and my sister is 4 years older than I am, but she never told me a thing. . . . I had to find out for myself. I put two and two together, like when I saw the paper and I saw the birth record. I figured, wow, they must sleep together. I found out the hard way.

> I went out there to my sister's farm to see her baby born, because I never saw a baby born.

Some women connected the secrecy surrounding biological processes with parental interference in their lives. As one never-married woman expressed it, the result of her parents' prudishness about sexuality was to delay her entrance into a nursing job:

> When I graduated from high school, I wanted to be a nurse. They didn't want me to be a nurse. It wasn't the proud profession that it is today . . . it wasn't a Florence Nightingale attitude. At least with my mother it wasn't . . . I don't know, seeing male patients bare or something.

In describing why she did not return to high school, another never-married woman cited her problem with menstruation. She was an only child, and her mother had bouts of mental illness. She recalled that her own sickness coincided with her mother's illnesses. These events during her teenage years maintained her dependence in the family:

> I had female trouble in high school. When I had my cycle, I would hemorrhage, dark blood, and it made me so weak. I took viosterol to build me up, and that helped me build up my weight and strength. They didn't have Kotex in those days, and women didn't carry big pocketbooks so I couldn't go to school. They used cheesecloths, called poseys, in those days, and you'd have to soak them and hang them out on the line to dry. It was an awful dirty mess.

Two other never-married women, both from large families, were disabled as young girls. The first perceived that her parents used her disability to keep her dependent on the family; she lived with her parents until they died when she was in her thirties. She contracted polio and described her childhood as confined and overprotected:

> The first time I tried to ride a bicycle, I fell off. That was the last of the bicycle. My parents were so afraid I was going to be hurt. But, of course, the other kids, when they learned to ride bicycles, they fell off, too! That didn't make any difference to my parents.... I was protected, no question about it. Like, the other kids had to work in the store, and they all hated it. But I couldn't. Now I think I probably could have just as well as the other kids, but my parents wouldn't let me, and it would have been good for me.

The other woman had a different experience with disability. After a severe injury as a child, she was determined to learn to walk with artificial legs:

> The Red Cross got my first pair of legs, and I learned to walk. They sent me crutches and they were brand new, but I got rid of them. I didn't want no crutches or nothing. My mother said I learned by holding onto furniture.... I never used a cane or anything. I used to walk so good that people thought I had polio or hip trouble and the legs didn't bother me at all.

Although several never-married women cited childhood diseases or disabilities as affecting their lives, none of the widows had this experience. The women did not blame their parents for their early dependence, but they did suggest that their parents used illness (either the parent's or the child's) to ensure that the child stay at home, long after they reached adulthood. Remaining "dependent" under such circumstances was very much a reciprocal relationship. The parents of several never-married women needed that particular child to remain at home, and those women were socialized toward their family's needs.

THE FAMILISTIC IDEOLOGY

In the 19th century, family relationships were based on a set of mutual obligations, where "parents raised and supported their children with the dual expectations that the children would start to work as soon as they were able and that they would ultimately support the parents in old age" (Hareven, 1977, p. 64). This familistic ideology facilitated the self-sufficiency of the household and fostered family survival during the process of industrialization, urbanization, and immigration. It was supported by social norms and customs that stressed the interdependence of individuals and their families. A widow in the present study captured the interdependence of the generations contained in the family ideal:

> My grandmother always taught me that the way I treated people when I was young is the way I would be treated when I was old.

Familism, an earlier form of social organization than individualism, emphasized collectivity (Acker, 1988; Laslett, 1972; Smith & Valenze, 1988). The familistic ideology was based on the organization of the household as a corporate entity (Hareven, 1987). The primary ties of 19th century families were not of sentiment as they are today, but of obligation, for the purpose of ensuring the autonomy and survival of the household (Bourdieu, 1976; Rosenberg, 1975). The household included the nuclear family of parents and their children, which was the preferred household structure during the 19th century, but it was a flexible unit, expanding and contracting to fit the needs of the family (Modell & Hareven, 1973). Especially for immigrants and working-class people, the household was likely to include kin and various nonrelatives such as boarders and lodgers.

In the long history of America's transformation from an agrarian economy to industrial capitalism, the familistic ideology was adapted from rural collective life to the new demands of a growing urban environment (Hareven, 1987). Immigrant groups used the familistic ideology as a survival strategy in migrating from Europe to North America (see also Hareven's [1982b] study of French Canadians; McLaughlin's [1971] study of Italian Americans in Buffalo; Scott and Tilly's [1975] study of European and American 19th century working-class families; and Tentler's [1979] synthesis of studies of industrial workers in the early 20th century). Although the family's grip on the decisions of individuals loosened over time, families were not passive reactors to change. The family acted as "an active agent, fostering social change and facilitating the adaptation of its members to new social and economic conditions" (Hareven, 1977, p. 58). Family survival depended on individuals to delay or sacrifice their personal desires. The family, acting as a broker between its members and the work site, held onto its power over individuals by determining when, where, and who would go to work and marry (Hareven, 1982b).

The ideal of individualism gradually came to replace familism (Scott & Tilly, 1975). Individualism, a philosophy rooted in the ideals of liberal moral theory from the English Enlightenment, emphasized the rights and conscience of the individual (Smith & Valenze, 1988). Arising first in 19th century middle-class families, contemporary norms of the family reflect the individualistic ideology of the family as a private, child-centered unit consciously separating itself from the harsh outside world (Hareven, 1987).

LIVING ON THE EDGE OF DEPENDENCY

The welfare state has emerged since the 19th century, along with the rise of individualism. Governmental regulation, such as Social Security, welfare benefits, and mandatory education, has penetrated the lives of most Americans, particularly the poor and working-class (Hareven, 1982a). Over the course of the 20th century, dependence on welfare has become a structural feature of working-class life (Katz, 1983). Individuals and families increasingly must rely on state services to survive. Women born in 1910 were among the first to experience the widespread reliance on public charity.

One third of the women in the study lost a parent during childhood. Experiences of early loss are shown in Table 4.2.

Their experiences reflect a demographic reality of 19th and early 20th century working-class life (Katz, 1975; Scott & Tilly, 1975; Uhlenberg, 1980). These families coped with the temporary or permanent loss of a breadwinner or caregiver by employing one of three survival strategies. In the first strategy, families struggled to keep the family of orientation together in the same household, even though such family autonomy was often impossible given the structural inequalities faced by these working-class people. In the second strategy, families depended on their connections to a wider kin network of grandparents, siblings, other relatives, and sometimes boarders. The kin network served as a safety net when parents died, became insti-

TABLE 4.2 Incidence of Parental Loss in Childhood

Marital Status:	Woman's Age At Loss:	Parent's Death:	Survival Strategies:
NM WOMEN:	Before Birth	Father	Mother took in boarders; sister sent to live with aunt
	1	Father	Mother worked in mill and took in laundry; sister quit school to work
	8	Father	Mother worked as waitress to support 2 children
	1	Mother	Sent to live with grandmother and aunt; taken back when father remarried
	2	Mother	Sent to orphanage for 16 years
	7	Mother	Sent to orphanage for 7 years; returned to father after he remarried
WIDOWS:	11	Father	Large family; older siblings were sent out to work
	15	Father	Sent to live with grandmother in rooming house
	2	Mother	Sent to live with various kin when father remarried
	10	Mother	Father kept family together

tutionalized, were separated from the family, or could no longer function in their roles, a finding that is consistent with other studies of working-class family life (see also Hareven, 1987; Langman, 1987; Rapp, 1982). In the third strategy, families relied on welfare institutions, such as orphanages, to care for their children. Uhlenberg (1980) found that orphanages were common in the 19th century and early 20th century. In 1900, about 24% of the children born would lose at least one parent to death before they reached age 15; one in 62 would lose both parents. To place these data in perspective, by 1976, only 5% of all children would lose a parent to death before age 15, while one in 1,800 would lose both parents. Unlike today, adoption into the kin network and placement in an orphanage were both common mechanisms to deal with the prevalence of orphanhood.

These strategies demonstrate the operation of the familistic ideology, but reveal, as well, how that ideology was changing to incorporate the rise of individualism and the welfare state that characterize industrial capitalism in the 20th century. The women described various consequences of being cared for by adults other than their parents for some portion of their early lives. Most women had close relationships with grandparents, aunts, older siblings, or nuns, but the few who did not were notable exceptions. They felt that the family's solution to parental loss was not in their best interest. Feelings of care and interdependence as well as feelings of neglect, abuse, loneliness, and hate went along with the temporary solution of being cared for by others. For them, individual and family needs conflicted. The purpose of the familistic ideology was to preserve the family at all costs, but this was not always possible. Thus, the concept of familism captures an ideology that is different from people's own assessments of family strategies. The beliefs of a given culture at a particular point in time should be examined along with actual behavior (Rosenberg, 1975). Providing life history data from participants of the relatively recent past allows for the examination of the tensions between individual and family needs. The women's testimonies of what happened to them as children provide their perspectives on the meaning of separation and loss and thus flesh out the familistic ideology and its consequences.

Keeping the Family of Orientation Together

To illustrate the operation of the familistic ideology when a parent died, the experiences of 3 women whose fathers died while they were children are described. Each situation was different, partly due to the size of the family of orientation. One never-married woman lost her father when she was 8 years old. Her mother worked as a waitress to support the 2 children, until the daughter graduated from high school and went to work to support herself and her mother. In this case, there were no extended kin available, but the small family size allowed them to manage to care for themselves. This woman's brother married and had children. She stayed with her mother until her mother's death.

The second situation is the experience of a widow who was the seventh of 10 children. Her father died when she was 11 years old. Her only older sister was already married and out of the house when her father died, so housework fell to her as their mother's assistant:

> My mother raised all of us, and she never worked out of the house. The kids all pitched in. The boys all had paper routes . . . and I was doing everything. I was helping in the house . . . and they all grew up and Thank God, they are all pretty good kids.

In the third case, a never-married woman whose father died when she was an infant described the changes her family went through to support themselves. She was the youngest of five children. When her father died, her mother went on welfare at first, but then got a job on a farm:

> She went on the farm picking hops for beer, and she used to do washing. She used to drag me along on the sled in the wintertime. . . . Oh, she had it hard, and my oldest sister got married at 17. She didn't help at all at home. . . . My other sister had to quit high school to go to work, and she got upset about that.

In other family situations, the experience of a parent's mental illness was absorbed by the family. The remaining parent supported the family during the other parent's temporary absence. One single woman described her mother as "off her trolley a little bit." An only child, she remained with her parents until they died in her seventh decade:

> Well, she always had kind of symptoms, even when I was little. You know, other people always told me that my mother was superstitious. Like those things that kids used to say, "Step on a crack and you'll break your mother's back." I think it was something that was kind of handed down in the family. Why it affected her, I really don't know. But I do know that she had a nervous breakdown before she was married. . . . We did send her away to see if anything could be done, but they said that she wasn't very bad and that she wasn't a nuisance to society, and they only kept her about 3 months. And then we took her back.

Another never-married woman described her father's bout with mental illness which resulted from seeing his own father shot dead.

He was sent to a sanitarium, and her mother did not allow him to come home:

> We think that some of his problems may have come from up there in that part of the country. There may have been the shortage of some chemical. . . . He was somebody who couldn't work for other people. He resented authority. . . . He had this streak in him, that he wouldn't assert himself. Whether it was that he lacked a chemical, I don't know.

The common experience among these women who temporarily lost a parent was that their immediate families handled the loss as best they could. They did not expect a cure from these illnesses. If the remaining parent was able to cope with supporting the household, intervention from extended kin or public charity was not required.

Surrogate Parents and Kin Support

In the second response to parental loss, grandparents and aunts substituted for parents by taking the children into their homes. For the widow who spent several periods of time in her grandmother's rooming house, her mother's institutionalization brought her back again:

> My mother and father separated for a while, never legally, and we all lived together in this rooming house. Then my mother got TB when my sister was born, and she had to go up to the sanitarium for a year. So, my grandmother had to take care of us. My aunt took my sister because she was ill, and my grandmother took my brother and I. I was only 8 and my brother was 11. She had to run the rooming house besides, and she took care of us, and we kinda looked up to her, as a mother really.

In another situation, however, a never-married woman's sister went to live with her aunt when her father died, and the aunt refused to send the child back. As a result of not growing up together, this woman did not develop a close relationship with her sister:

> After my father died, and I was born, my sister was taken very sick and she went into convulsions, so my aunt wanted to help my mother, and she took my sister. At that time, just after my father died, my

mother was sort of at loose ends, and she had a house full of boarders, and she had to take care of us. . . . Well, it was just one of those circumstances. But afterwards, my mother realized what she had done, and she told her she wanted my sister back, but my aunt said "I won't give her up, she's like my own," and her husband refused, too.

Another never-married woman's mother died when she was an infant. She was given to her grandmother and aunt, who cared for her until her father remarried a year later. Then, she was raised by her father and step-mother. Her domineering father and step-mother favored the son they had together. Her father lived until he was 94 years old; she said she never got away from him.

For one widow, her mother's death resulted in her description of a tragic childhood. She was placed with relatives who abused her. She had to work for her room and board by sweeping, cleaning, and doing laundry. She lived with her grandparents, an aunt, an older sister, all in different homes, until she graduated from high school and was able to support herself:

My mother died when I was 2 years old, and then my father remarried and my step-mother didn't want his children around, even my oldest brother who paid his board.

Apart from living with an older sister, this woman lost touch with her four other living siblings. Two brothers were sent to a work house for orphaned boys, and her younger sister was adopted by another family.

The disorganizing effect of a mother's death was evident in the above cases. Although the familistic ideology was clearly operating during these periods of parental loss, family solutions were not always made with the interests of the particular child in mind, and they were not typically favorable experiences. Yet, the value of family autonomy was reinforced strongly, leaving a legacy of caregiving roles. Never-married women became surrogate mothers themselves, and widows cared for children and grandchildren.

Recourse to Public Charity

Finally, some families resorted to welfare institutions to help them cope with the loss of a parent. In these families, it was the mother's death or absence that prompted the need for outside help. Two of the never-married women were raised in a Catholic orphanage. After her mother died when she was 2 years old, one woman and her only sibling went to live at the orphanage. She thought of her father more as a friend who would visit her and look after her. Living at the orphanage was a wonderful experience for her, and regarding her situation of growing up without a mother, she noted:

> I enjoyed it there very much, because it was the only life I knew. What you didn't have, you couldn't miss. So, actually I had 10 or 12 mothers in the nuns.

She stayed at the orphanage until she graduated from high school. The other never-married woman who lived at the orphanage, however, did not spend as long a time there. Her mother died when she was 7 years old, and she and her older siblings stayed with their father for a few years. They came to the attention of the authorities because they were unsupervised while her father worked at night, and through a court order, they were sent to the orphanage. When her father remarried 6 years after her mother's death, she went to live with him and his second wife, whom she hated.

One widow's family experience with mother absence was another variation. She was the fifth child in a family of 11, and when her parents divorced and her mother left home, the experience was different for her and the older children from what it was for the younger children. The four youngest were placed in the county orphan's home where they lived until they finished school. The older children were already out of the house and on their own. However, she was 14 years old and just starting high school. Several of her sisters close to her age had to quit school and go to work, but her age at the time of the divorce and her birth order favored her remaining in school. Through the intervention of the county social services department and a professional women's service organization, the impact of her mother's absence was not as traumatic as it could have been under different circumstances:

> We had social services, women who came to visit my mother and help out once in a while with welfare, and there were two sisters who worked rather closely together. . . . They knew I had graduated from elementary school, and they wanted to help me through high school,

and she agreed. She'd like to see me go to high school. They bought all of my books, all of my supplies, and they bought me a winter coat one winter when I didn't have one. I remember it cost $27, and it was gray, and it was long, and it was warm, and I was very proud of that coat, and I sat down and wrote them a letter thanking them for what they had done for me so far in my life.

These experiences are consistent with three characteristics of working-class family life in the early part of the 20th century: nuclear family units employed various strategies to maintain their autonomy, the kin network was a resource that exercised power over the lives of individuals, and welfare institutions were utilized by working-class families. As children during the Progressive Era, some of these working-class women came to the attention of middle class reformers and public authorities. On the one hand, some women expressed gratitude for the intervention from others who were not their own parents. Others, however, expressed resignation about their fate. On balance, these experiences suggest the complexity of family life as well as the pain that often accompanies severed family ties and the absence of a mother's physical presence. The normative prescription was that families took care of their own. The reality was much more complex. Families did take care of their own, but some did so begrudgingly or poorly. Recourse to charity befell the less fortunate, in situations where fathers could not or would not assume responsibility, where there were few available kin, or where there were too many children left at home.

SUMMARY

These women inherited a legacy of hard work, personal sacrifice, mystification about the reality of adult womanhood, and a marginal place in an industrial society. They shared a common culture as daughters of working-class families. Many lost parents either temporarily or permanently, and their families sought solutions within a hierarchy of options: first within the nuclear family, next within the wider kin network, and finally, as a last resort, through public agencies. They were socialized to expect to work hard, and they were not prepared realistically for biological processes. They learned to value the autonomy of the family unit, and as the next chapter reveals, to delay choices to become independent if their labor or support was needed by the family of orientation. They also learned that family life is full of contradictions, and rather than paint a rosy picture of what happened to them, they recounted and assessed their lives in realistic terms.

5

Pathways in Young Adulthood: Remaining Single and Becoming Married

In becoming young adults, the women in the study began to differentiate. The members of one group fulfilled the expectations for women to establish a family of procreation. They married, had children, became grandmothers, and eventually lost their husbands to death. The other group did not follow these normative expectations. They remained single, and for the most part, maintained close ties to their families of orientation. This chapter examines the meaning of the transition to adulthood within the context of remaining single or getting married for women from the 1910 birth cohort. Three pathways were followed, and within each pathway, some expression of family need or personal choice was evident. The three pathways are summarized in Table 5.1.

Ten women married relatively "on time," between the ages of 18 and 24. They left their childhood families to establish their own families. Five women married later, between the ages of 26 and 30. By remaining with their parents, they delayed marriage until "it was almost too late." Their experiences as young adults were more comparable to the never-married women, while on-time marriage and delayed marriage differentiated the widowed group during their twenties. As a whole, widows did not become more distinct from the never-married group until middle age, after their marriages were well underway. Finally, 15 women did not marry at all.

TABLE 5.1 Pathways to Marriage and Lifelong Singlehood

		Total
ON-TIME MARRIAGE, Ages 18-24:		10
Escape from mistreatment or hard work	7	
All my friends were getting married	3	
DELAYED MARRIAGE, Ages 26-30:		5
I was needed at home	4	
I was enjoying the single life	1	
THE PROCESS OF NOT GETTING MARRIED:		15
My mother needed me	6	
I had to take care of myself	4	
Broken hearts	2	
I had other things I wanted to do	3	
	Total	30

MARRYING ON TIME

Family composition was a major factor in the experience of marrying on schedule, as shown in Table 5.2.

None of the widows were the last born child in their families of orientation, yet 5 never-married women were. The widows tended to be either first borns or middleborns and from larger families. Seven of the 10 women who married on time were middleborns, and 8 of them came from families with 5 to 11 children. Although the never-married women were most likely to be the only available female child left to care for one or both parents, the widows who married on schedule had the opportunity and the motivation to leave. Consistent with Rubin's (1976) working-class study, the women in this sample saw marriage as an escape from drudgery and mistreatment in their parent's home, and it was supported by the choices of their friends. Two patterns were found in these 10 lives, as shown in Table 5.1.

Marriage as Escape from Mistreatment or Hard Work

Seven women discussed getting married in the context of leaving behind family situations where they were mistreated or

TABLE 5.2 Family of Orientation Composition

	Never-Married Women	Widows	Total
Only child	1	1	2
Oldest child	5	4	9
Middle child: oldest girl	2	3	5
only girl, with brothers	1	0	1
older & younger siblings	1	7	8
Youngest child	5	0	5
Total	15	15	30

NOTE: Five never-married women were the only daughter in their families, in contrast to one widow, and she was an only child.

there was too much work to do. Three women described growing up in unhappy homes with fathers who were cruel or distant. One oldest daughter of four children described how her social life was restricted by her father. She began to date her husband at age 17, graduated from high school, and went to work as a salesclerk:

> So, I didn't do too much, like I said, my father was strict. I had to sneak out on dates. . . . All my life I had an inferiority complex because I was so short and sheltered by my father. . . . I got married to get out of the house.

Another woman was the oldest of six children. Her parents were divorced when she was 18, but her father was a "womanizer" and was out of the house since the time she was 11. Her family needed her income so she quit school after the tenth grade and worked as a salesclerk. She married at 18 to get away from home, despite the objections of her mother and mother-in-law:

> When I got married, I don't remember that far back because too many people disapproved. We just eloped. I didn't have a wedding, but it was a very happy time. Life goes on.

Her independence was temporary because she and her husband lived with her mother for a year after they were married so that she could continue to take care of her younger siblings while her mother worked. Then, her first child was born, and they went to live with her husband's family.

A third woman, whose childhood was an extreme case of physical abuse and emotional neglect, lived with relatives after her mother died when she was 2 years old. She graduated from high school and was left to take care of herself. She worked in a laundry and married at age 22:

> I didn't have any love as a child, but I got love from my husband. I can't understand a woman not wanting to have children because I couldn't wait to have my own. I took care of other people's children from the time I was 7 years old, and I wanted my own.

Three other women wanted to escape from the drudgery of helping to support or care for their siblings. One woman, whose parents were Italian immigrants, was the oldest of seven children. She completed the eighth grade, and at age 14 went to work as a field hand "apple picking and onion topping." She also helped her mother at home with the younger children: "We all did hard labor, back-breaking work." She married at age 21, and "then life began."

Another woman described her marriage as a liberation from her childhood years. She was the 7th of 10 children, and her father died when she was 11. She completed high school and worked as a sales-clerk until she married at age 23:

> When I got married, it was an entirely different life. I was free to do with my life what I wanted to do. Nobody was telling me what had to be done today. So, I was an emancipated woman. I mean it! With my large family and there wasn't much money in the house, so we had to do everything ourselves, and I was the one who had to do most of it. I never resented it, but I didn't realize until I got married what I did do before. It was an entirely different type of a life for me . . . somebody cared about me. I didn't have to do this for that one, or something for another. Somebody now tried to do things for me, and I just immediately enjoyed it.

Another woman described herself as the "gypsy of the family" because she was the only one of 10 children to leave the town in which she was raised. She was the ninth child and was sent to boarding school at age 14 because she showed academic promise. Since her family was poor, she lived in the matron's home and worked for her room and board. She married at 20 after she completed high school and nurse's training:

> When I was a nurse, I envied every maternity patient. I couldn't wait to get pregnant, and I was married 3 weeks when I got pregnant. Oh, I just couldn't wait.

Being a wife and mother was her central ambition because she wanted a life of her own—one that was more exciting than her mother's life had been. Her parents were elderly when she was young, and she did not want to return home to take care of them. Her alternative was to move away, marry, and raise her own family:

> Ours was a happy marriage. You know one big reason for that was after we had the two boys, he had a vasectomy. I'm telling you the truth, those worries were gone. You see, that can affect a marriage. I worried because we were very poor and my mother had 10, and I said, "what can I do?" and she said, "would I have had 10 if I had known?!".... I'll tell you, after that, it was one great big honeymoon. Don't let anybody kid you that marriage can't be beautiful and fulfilling. It was beautiful.

Finally, for one woman, marriage was a second choice. She was the oldest of 5 children and did not get along with her mother. She graduated from high school at 16, joined a convent, and stayed for a year and a half.

> I loved everything about it, and I never did really know why I came home. It wasn't my idea. The sisters just told me one day, "your father is in the parlor, and you are going home." They didn't give me any reasons. I applied to go back in 3 months, but they said no, that I had been with boys in the summer. Well, I had. I ran around with the same crowd I went to high school with, and my high school friends graduated the month after I came home. I had already finished my studies the year before.... The nuns didn't think I was behaving as befitting a nun. I really wanted to go back.... They didn't ask me, they just told me I was going. I had no idea. I think now that it was just because God had other plans for me. Because the kind of life I have had has been so varied, and I have been with so many people, and I know I have touched a lot of people, more than I would have at the convent.

When she returned home, she taught school for 2 years, then married at age 21. For her, marriage was a second choice in relation to her preferred career as a nun. When she was prevented from that choice, she fell back on a more traditional option.

Marriage Timing and the Influence of Friends

Three women set the context in which they married in terms of what their girlfriends were doing at the time; they married within a year of their best friends. Although other women said they married because "it was the thing to do," each of the women below lost a parent before the age of 15. The first woman had two siblings, and her father died when she was 15. She graduated from high school and went to work as a clerk. She married in 1935, just before she was 24:

> We got married secretly, because where I worked, you weren't supposed to be married. . . . I don't know why or what their idea was then, but afterwards, I got pregnant, so I had to leave. . . . I had gone with another boy, but he was Jewish and I liked him very much, but my husband was Catholic and my girlfriend, my oldest girlfriend that I went to kindergarten with, she and I and her husband now, too, we went together, see, and I got married a year before she did. Then, she got married the next year. Oh, yes, I was in love, or I probably wouldn't have put up with all I did.

Her experience indicated the influence of normative and situational factors on her decision to marry her husband. Both were Irish Catholics, and others in her peer group followed the expectations for young women to marry.

A second woman described a similar experience. Her mother, whom she described as an "old-fashioned mother," died when she was 10, when four of her seven siblings were still at home. They were raised by her father, who was strict but loving. She quit school at age 14:

> I just wanted to leave. My father said I could if I wasn't going to be happy in school. But, everybody did it then. All my friends did, too. The girlfriend I ran around with, her and I both quit at the same time, and we went together to continuation school until I was 16. Then, I got out, and I worked a little while. I didn't have no job or education for a job.

She married at age 19. Like her mother, she became an "old-fashioned mother" and never worked outside the home again:

> Like all my friends got married, because we all hung around together. I was the first one in my group to get married. And, then, they all spoiled my baby. They used to come to the house, and I was the only one with a baby. But, then, eventually, they got children, too, so our lives were all the same.

The third woman was the 5th of 11 children. Her parents divorced when she was 14, but she was able to complete high school through the assistance of a professional women's organization. She described the events that led to her marriage in normative terms:

> I always wanted to be married. I dated quite a few boys. . . . I always felt that marriage was the thing for all girls. I think girls of my era did feel that we should be married. My closest girlfriend and I got to be very good friends for the 4 years of high school. We graduated together. She started to date about the same time I started to date. She married, and I was her bridesmaid. They were married in June, and we were married in November, and she was my bridesmaid. She had a very wonderful life . . . and I had a wonderful married life, all the way through.

"ALMOST AN OLD MAID"

For the 5 women who married late, the pathway to marriage was a process of almost not marrying. Their experiences foreshadow what happened to the never-married women as family events or personal desires delayed marriage. Like the widows discussed above and the never-married women discussed later, some element of family need or personal choice was evident in almost being "an old maid." As Table 5.1 shows, 4 of these women were needed at home, but one chose to be single until 29.

"I Was Needed at Home"

The first woman, who married at age 29, was the 7th of 11 children. Her older siblings were already married, and she was still at home caring for her parents, who were both elderly and sick. She quit school at age 16 and did not go to work. Her role was to stay at home in the family of orientation:

> Well, I thought there for a while I was going to be an old maid because I was 29. There again, I was close to my mother. I took care of her, and when she died of cancer, I was home.

A second woman described several events which delayed her marriage to the man she dated when she was 18. Her parents were unhappily married, and her mother exerted a great deal of influence over her:

> My mother never approved of him. She always called him "good time Charlie." See, he was a lot like my father. He loved life. Two weeks before we were to get married, we broke up. So, then I didn't see him for 9 years until my father died, when he came to pay his respects to my father. So, in the meantime, I was going out with other fellows, but I was such an old maid. I pulled every fellow apart, it was a shame . . . but they bored me to death. So, when he came back to pay his respects to my father, we made up, and we went out and got married the following year, and we had 37 very happy years.

This woman worked from the time she graduated from high school, and she still works today. She was the oldest of three daughters, and she expected she would become an "old maid":

> My sister had a lot of boyfriends, and she used to kid me and say "Oh, you're going to be an old maid." And my husband use to tease me and tell the boys he kept me from the old maids' home because I was 28 when we got married.

The third woman described a similar experience with a domineering mother who did not want her to marry. She was an only child, and her parents fought bitterly during their married life. She graduated from high school and went to work. She dated several men, but did not get the courage to disobey her mother until she was 30 years old:

> She was always demoting me, and I got a terrible complex. And, I stuttered. I mean I could not talk. I just couldn't. It was a handicap, but

you can see I got over it when I got away from her. . . . I lived with her a year when I got married because she couldn't part with me. She liked my husband immensely before we were married. I was going to have a party and announce my engagement, and my girlfriend said "you know darn well she'll never marry him" because I had had a lot of dates. But then, I went with him for years, so I got mad. I said, "I'll show 'em, we'll get married anyway." So, we were gonna have a party, and my mother raised Holy Cain. She didn't want me to have the party. She didn't want me to get married. But see, I was 30, and I thought if I don't marry this guy, I mean everybody should get married, and I liked him immensely. I mean, I loved him. So, there was no point in not getting married. Well, anyway, she was domineering, very domineering. I think at this late date I should have married the guy I went with before I met my husband. But he was divorced, maybe 12 years before, and she didn't go for that.

Her marriage was an escape from an unhappy family of orientation. Like the first 2 widows, she was "saved from the old maids' home."

A fourth woman also came from an unhappy home, where she "never saw any love in the house." She had an older brother in an institution. She stated she did not want to marry because her brother's illness was inherited. After graduating from high school, she worked as a waitress and had an active social life. Her father was killed when she was 21. After refusing marriage proposals from other men, she met her husband:

I loved him. I hadn't intended to get married. I was 26, and I could have married long before that. But, when I saw a guy get too, you know, as if he had firm intentions of asking me to marry him, I would very politely give him the air, shall we say. . . . I told him my whole background, and he said it didn't matter, but it did matter. . . . I got the feeling that he married me to have a family. I didn't marry for that reason.

"I Was Enjoying the Single Life"

Finally, the fifth woman married late, at age 29, because she was enjoying "the single life." She was the fourth of seven children, and lived at home until she married. Unlike the other women who married late, her parents were Italian immigrants, and they always had a "happy home." She described the years before she married as the happiest time in her life, and she did so by comparing her single status to her married sisters:

> I didn't get married when I was young, so, I really enjoyed myself. I went all over, compared to my sisters, who married when they were 21. I went out more than my sisters ever did. I went on trips, and they didn't. . . . I was married in 1942, and it had to be between '32 and '42. I had a little money because I was working more than they ever worked. I worked most of my life. I worked when I was single, and I went back to work during the wartime, and then my children were born, and then after my husband died, I went back to work. So, I really worked quite a bit in my life. But, you know, that is good for you, too. . . . I really enjoyed working, and my sisters used to say that it was more of a social life for me. I made friends, and I would always go early in the morning before work, and we would have breakfast, and coffee, and enjoy ourselves, and then go in to work. It was really exciting.

THE PROCESS OF NOT GETTING MARRIED

Each never-married woman described the process by which she did not get married. The road to permanent singlehood was a hidden event (Brim & Ryff, 1980) in the female life course. The process by which these women did not marry consisted of a series of events and transitions during their childhood and young adulthood that cut across several life course careers. Some combination of events related to their family, friends, education, work, residence, and health interacted to limit their opportunity or desire to marry. The never-married women demonstrated four patterns, as shown in Table 5.1.

"My Mother Needed Me"

For 6 never-married women, their family of orientation came first in their lives. Two of these women grew up in mother-only households after their fathers died when they were very young. As the youngest child in the family, they were expected to go to work as soon as they graduated from high school. They both took clerical jobs and had an uninterrupted work history of 45 years. They lived with and supported their mothers financially until their mothers died:

> I had to take my mother into consideration. No, I couldn't do anything. She had to be my prime concern. . . . I don't think I was college material. I might have gone to business school, had we been able to afford it. . . . I wanted to get to work, because I knew we needed the money. So there was just no question about it. . . . It was my responsibility because my older brother was married, and my other brother was in school, so I was elected.

> I was single, so naturally she lived with me. . . . I just took care of her. I made sure she had enough money to get along.

Three of the women who stayed at home to be of service to their families of orientation could not find work during the period in which their mothers needed them, from the mid 1920s to the early 1930s. All 3 of these women were raised in two-parent homes where their fathers worked. Two did not complete high school because they were "sickly," and the third graduated from high school and business school, yet did not go to work until several years later. However, she had been a sickly and protected child. The employment opportunities of these women were also interrupted because their mothers were sick. All 3 stayed at home until their parents died. These women did not have friends their own age; their lives were centered around their parents. One was an only child, the second was an only daughter, and the third was the only girl left at home after her sisters married or went to work:

> My parents were my whole life. . . . She was quite bad when I was in high school, and that probably contributed some to the fact that I didn't go on. See, I told you I wasn't very well when I was young. . . . They were basically years when I was just sort of stuck with my mother, and I didn't have too many young friends.

> We were always together. We enjoyed going out around together. She was very close to me, and I was very close to her. . . . I never liked school. . . . I was sick a lot, and I was kept back, and it was hard for me to catch up.

> There was just that prejudice against Catholics and Jews. None of us got jobs, so I went back home. I probably would have stayed at what

they called The Club. . . . It was a nice place for a working girl. . . . I went home, and my father said my mother needed me because she wasn't too well then so I helped with the housework.

The sixth woman who remained in her parent's home because she was needed was the oldest daughter of 11 children. She felt responsible for her siblings because her mother was "always sickly." She was "never told" that she had to fill in for her mother. She just "automatically did it." After she graduated from high school, she stayed at home for 5 years, taking care of the house and the children. She also lived with her mother all her life because she said she was the only one her mother would allow to take care of her:

> See, I wasn't prepared to do anything out of school. I was going to be a teacher, with all my girlfriends. I didn't go to normal school, but they all did. I stayed at home because I didn't take a business course. That is how I decided to take hairdressing. And I thought I've got to do something with my own life. See, I brought the children up, and I used to take care of the house and make up the beds. See, my mother was never too well. She had very serious operations. I thought we were going to lose her so many times. . . . That is why I stayed home so much. . . . She didn't like to go anywhere because she would say I would be left alone at home. . . . That was her excuse so she didn't have to stay anywhere because she just wanted to stay with me.

"I Had to Take Care of Myself"

There were 4 never-married women who described the process by which they did not marry in terms of their own financial needs. After their mothers died when they were young, 2 were raised in an orphanage. Both were youngest daughters whose older siblings eventually married and started their own families. One of them lived for a year with her father and step-mother, but she was not wanted, and she ran away from home at age 16. She quit school in the eighth grade because she had to go to work to support herself. She went to work as a live-in housekeeper for families from 1925 to 1952, and after that, she worked as a store clerk and lived alone for the rest of her life:

> I have always had it hard, terrible hard, and when I came here, and saw my little apartment, I felt as if I was in seventh heaven. Every-

thing was new and I made friends, and it was mine. Nobody can take it away from me.

The other woman who was raised in the orphanage had quite a different experience. She went there at age 2 and stayed until she graduated from high school. She was the nuns' "pet" and thought of them as mothers. Her experience in the orphanage probably contributed to her lifelong singlehood. She attributed to the nuns her happy memories of childhood, good education, sense of purpose in life, and faith:

> Oh, they must have had a pretty good influence, because they was the ones that imparted my faith to me, you know, because no one else could, and I've stayed a staunch Catholic ever since.

The nuns were her role models. They were celibate and religious. By growing up in an orphanage with 200 other girls, she did not learn to keep house. She did learn that she had to take care of herself. After leaving the orphanage, she went to business school and to work. She stayed at the same job until her retirement 45 years later. She lived with other single women until 1955, and then she lived alone.

The other 2 women who had to take care of themselves led similar lives. Both grew up in large families and were the oldest daughters. They quit school in 1925 and went to work as live-in housekeepers for wealthier families. Then, in 1942, when more factory jobs were open to women, they obtained better jobs. Both retired in 1968. They returned home for short periods of time during their adult years when they were needed. Otherwise, they lived alone and described their lives as having to fend for themselves.

Broken Hearts

Two never-married women recalled their early adult years as a time when friends were getting married, but they were not. One woman described a series of events and transitions which pointed to the process of not getting married. Her own mother died when she was a baby. She was raised by her step-mother and domineering father who "always kept me under heel." Her parents told her she was clumsy and stupid. She perceived that their harsh assessment of her kept her from graduating from high school:

> I had a hard time getting through school. Then it seemed that everybody was getting married, and I was still plodding along, but then after a while, when I got out and was doing baby work, I found out I wasn't as stupid as I was painted. . . . I felt like I was kind of jumping a hurdle by getting away from my family.

However, before she went to work, she was engaged at age 18 to a young man who was killed:

> He accidentally fell down an elevator shaft. It was tragic. I went with people afterwards, but I never found anyone.

In spite of her tragedy and the problems at home, she stayed with her parents until their recent deaths. She spent most of her life in service to her unappreciative and demanding parents. Their need for her caregiving services was painfully reinforced in their socialization practices that kept her dependent and at home.

The second woman also experienced several tragedies in her early life. She described an uphill struggle to overcome the circumstances beyond her control. Her father died when she was a baby, and her older, never-married sister supported the family. At age 3, she had a disabling accident. She graduated from high school and business school, but did not go to work until the age of 43, possibly because she received a settlement from the accident. Her early adult years were spent dating and socializing with friends. Yet, her heart was broken when her fiance married someone else. She said she always loved him:

> Oh, sure, all these years, I've had other dates, but not like him. I didn't care about them, you know what I mean? He was the only man, my girlfriend can tell you that, boy, she knows.

"I Had Other Things I Wanted to Do"

Finally, 3 never-married women said that they wanted to accomplish something in their lives, and getting married was not the way they wanted to do it. All 3 women were career-oriented, which was atypical of other members of the sample. Two graduated from normal school, a three-year teacher training program. One woman became a teacher, but the other received further training as a licensed practical nurse and pursued a nursing career. The third woman graduated from high school and was employed as a secretary. During World War II, she enlisted in the Navy because:

> When you are that much younger, you love activity, and you can't miss a thing.

The other 2 women described a similar sense of adventure and excitement about their lives when they were young:

> I had places to go and things to see. And I wasn't going to be stopped, nobody was going to. It took me a long time to get going, but I made it.

> Ah, for many people, events like graduating and that sort of thing are very exciting, but as I say, the ends of things are not exciting to me. Its the getting there that's what interests me. I remember some particular days in my life, but a lot of them had to do with nature. The very good days.

All 3 of these women lived with members of their families of orientation throughout their lives. The secretary was a youngest daughter whose parents died before she was 25. She lived with her sister, brother-in-law, niece and nephew until she was 47, then moved to her own apartment. The other 2 women lived with their parents throughout adulthood. They were healthy throughout childhood and found "friends" in their family.

However, each of them had a different perspective on men, dating, and marriage. The teacher graduated from high school at age 15. After normal school, she went directly to work. She noted that once she got started on something, she had to go through with it:

> You see, teaching to me was not only a vocation but it was a hobby, too. Teaching, to me, was my life. Not that I was that good a teacher, but it is associated with books, too, and books to me are extremely important because books are my friends and trees are my friends, both of them. You can never be lonely really because you meet all kinds of people in books and have all kinds of experiences and learn

about the past experiences. I'm not so much interested in the future ones, that's all.

She said she did not have the opportunity to socialize, but on the other hand, "parties bore me to death." A transition occurred in her life when her sister married in 1933, reflecting her realization that in contrast to her married sister, she would remain single. She devoted herself to teaching some 1,200 children over the next 40 years.

> My sister and I used to always say that we were going to have children even if we had to adopt them. And then she got married, and the first year she got married, I wasn't going anywhere because I had been used to going out with her, and I was somewhat shy. It's hard to believe now! So, toward the end of the year, I thought to myself, "this is going to be the rest of your life." So, I thought I might as well get with it. From then on, I wasn't shy. So, I did things.

The nurse spoke about dating experiences in her early twenties. She said she did not know what was keeping her from "settling down," but she later went on to travel in various parts of the world:

> I never had good luck, I had some stinkers. They didn't turn me against men universally. Nothing ever came of any. I think there was one or two, that under different circumstances and under a different life, that might have. But, I had a lot of fun. I had a lot of different kinds and shapes and forms of men in my life, nothing that ever got down to the real serious, where I'd want to give up anything for something that I was not sure of.

The secretary noted that although she dated regularly, she just wasn't interested in marriage and childbearing:

> Because I have dated so many men all my life. When I was very young, a lot of gals used to say to me just to go out with one fella because marriage was the goal in life. But, it never was my answer in life, I'll tell you. But then they'd say, "Well, if you fell in love, you would have gotten married." My sister used to say, "you'd find a flaw even if it was in their necktie."

Thus, for these 3 women, their own goals in life took priority over the traditional roles most women pursued. They were the most educated in the sample, and although they came from working-class backgrounds, their own achievements in life suggest a middle-class orientation. On the other hand, 2 of them reside in subsidized apartments, and the third shares her apartment with her mother, circumstances which reflect a limited income. Their family of orientation responsibilities were important but did not overshadow their own desires for occupational achievement and personal independence. All of them remained closely connected to their families.

SUMMARY

These women, born in 1910, inherited a working-class background that had implications for the values they retained throughout life. The women described a complex web of events and processes in their early adult years. The events and characteristics of their family, friendship, work, health, and residence histories were interwoven. They organized the story of their own lives within the context of their families. They described how their biography intersected with their family's history to structure their opportunities to marry or remain single. In spite of similar background and socialization, the pathways they followed as adults differentiated in young adulthood. Half of them married, and half of them remained single.

Most of the women who married did so because they had the opportunity. Only one woman felt that marriage was a second choice for her. Otherwise, the women married, just their friends did, and often to escape an unhappy home. For the most part, those who married early did so because there was no one stopping them. Women who delayed or avoided marriage altogether did have something more pressing to do. Some of the women who did not marry emphasized their isolation from peers and their overriding family responsibility to work or care for parents. An exception to this pattern was the 3 never-married women who felt that marriage was not their answer in life. What they wanted to do was not defined by their families. Their lives were no less demanding or full of responsibility as young people than other women in the study. Rather, their families did not assert as much control over their life course decisions, affording them more opportunity to vary from the norms of married motherhood or parent care.

From the three pathways described in this chapter—marrying on time, marrying late, or remaining single—it is evident that in each one, women's opportunities to marry or to remain single were mediated by some combination of family need and personal choice. The family, through the process of socialization, exercised its value of familial self-sufficiency through these strategies, and the women's pathways suggest how they attended to the various demands. For these working-class daughters from the 1910 cohort, the family had a powerful role in structuring their life course transitions: some were sent out to work or to care for relatives at home and others were sent out to marry and reproduce. A few managed to carve out their own careers independent of family demands, but they, too, retained their family connections.

6

The Middle Years: Taking Care of Families

During their middle years, all of the women were involved in caregiving roles and responsibilities, which varied in terms of their family subcareers. Caregiving occurred primarily in relation to parents, husbands, and children. In this chapter, the family keeping strategies of never-married women are explored in relation to the family extensions of ever-married mothers.

TAKING CARE OF PARENTS

The experiences of never-married women and widows in this study were distinct in terms of the adult child/aging parent subcareer of the family life course (Feldman & Feldman, 1975). Parent caring was a primary family subcareer for the never-married women but not the widows. Twelve never-married women assumed major responsibilities for the care of one or both parents during their adult years, and only 4 widows did so. Moreover, 8 never-married women reached the age of 51 with at least one parent alive. Only 4 widows still had a parent living by that age. The never-married women were far more connected to their families of orientation throughout adulthood than the widows were. With few exceptions, once women married, they transferred their responsibilities to their families of procreation. This pattern is consistent with the Western European marriage strategy (Dixon, 1978; Watkins, 1984) of 19th and early 20th century working-class women and the role of "maiden aunt" of early 19th century American spinsterhood (Chambers-Schiller, 1984).

Never-Married Women and Their Parents

Only 3 never-married women did not assume the major responsibility for their parents during adulthood. Two of these women lost their mothers early in life and were raised in an orphanage. They lost their fathers, as well, through death or estrangement while they were in their early twenties. The parents of the third woman died before she was 24. The remaining 12 women played major roles in taking care of one or both parents. The women's responsibilities depended upon how long their parents lived. Four women provided short-term assistance, and the remaining 8 were fully involved in their parents' lives throughout adulthood. Table 6.1 displays these patterns.

Short-term care. While they were still in their thirties, 2 women provided nursing care for their mothers. One woman lived at home and did not work. She was 32 when her mother died:

> When my mother took ill, I took care of her. Fifteen months, she was bedridden. My sister had to work, and I took care of her. Then, she died after 15 months. She wouldn't let anybody give her the bedpan but me. My oldest sister couldn't even get near her.

The second woman lived at home, worked, and provided financial and nursing care to both parents, who died when she was 33. Her parents were ill for about 10 years. Both of these women had been disabled in childhood, and their early adult years were characterized by illness. Family obligations, as well, kept these women close to home. They were elected to be the child to stay at home with their parents and to nurse and care for them because other siblings were already married or working. Both of these women had another unmarried sister who worked to support the family. This type of total care, characterized by sharing a residence and providing financial support and physical care for parents, was typical of a later born daughter.

Two other women provided short-term assistance to their parents at times when they were needed. Their responsibilities to their families of orientation ceased when their parents died. Both women were the oldest child from a large family, and unlike the 2

TABLE 6.1 Parent Caregiving by Marital Status

Marital Status	No Care	Short-term Care	Lifelong Care	Total
Never-married women	3*	4	8	15
Widows	11**	3	1	15
Total	14	7	9	30

*The parents of these women died by the time they were 24.
**The age range of these widows when parents died during adulthood was greater: 21 to 64.

women above, they achieved an early independence from their families by leaving home to go to work. Still, they provided financial assistance and occasional personal care. This type of short-term assistance is evident in the example below where a woman arranged for her parents' funerals:

I bought her tombstone and my father's tombstone, and took pictures of them to show her so that she knew where she was going to be buried. And, sometimes, I think more now than I did at first because I had everything to do, you know, my father's furniture, his funeral. He gave me all this money so I could bury him, and my sister says, "I don't want to know anything." So, my brother put the furniture in storage, and I paid for the storage for 6 months, then I took it out and certain things that he had designated he wanted to give this one and that one, I gave it to them and all the other stuff I had piled on top of me, and I had to get rid of it the best I could.

Full involvement. The remaining 8 women lived with one or both of their parents all their lives, until their parents died. Only one of these women was not responsible financially for her parents at some point in her life; she never worked outside the home. She assumed all household and nursing responsibilities for her mother during the last 10 years of her mother's life. When she was 64, her mother died, and this event was the low point of her life:

Well, I did a little bit of everything; I was a nurse, cooking, cleaning, going to the store, dressing, undressing her. That kept me kind of busy. Buying groceries. I was busy every minute . . . I felt terrible. I naturally would. I was very lonely. . . . I really never got over it.

Another woman was only financially responsible for her mother. Yet, they had a reciprocal living/working relationship. The mother took care of the home, and the woman went out to work every day:

> My brother always said she did everything but feed me. She did all the cooking. I should have had her teach me some of the things, but I was just so used to having her ready for me when I come home, to sit down to the meal. So, she spoiled me that way, I guess . . . I probably didn't appreciate it at the time, but I do more now. I look back and realize how good it was, when you have to get your own meals. I hate to cook anyways.

As the adult child/aging parent subcareer lengthened, new dimensions were added to the women's caregiving roles, and their parents' deaths had greater meaning to them. For example, one woman, who lived with her mother, supported her financially, and served as her confidant, was deeply affected by her mother's death:

> She was 82. She had lived her life, and I was so grateful I had been able to keep her home because so many people get to a point where they can't be taken care of at home. Oh, it took me months to get over coming home to an empty house. It's an awful feeling. I'd expect her to be sitting in that chair. . . . I missed her terrible and it took months. That was in July, and then the following spring, I found another apartment because I wanted to get out of there, and . . . the day I came home from the funeral, I started packing all her clothes, oh, I got to get them out of here.

She transferred her caregiving services to an elderly aunt and uncle for whom she now shops and cooks. The depth of feeling expressed over the loss of her mother—her companion and confidant for most of her life—was the same expressed by some of the widows for their husbands.

The loss of a parent, however, gave women who lived with their parents all their lives their first sense of independence. At age 62, the woman below felt like an adult for the first time in her life:

> Well, I lost one, and then it was a year and a half before I lost the other one. It was awful that year and a half with my mother. I couldn't do much with her. I wasn't working at the same time. I told you that I lost my job at the same time that I lost my father. And I never went back to

work. . . . Well, it came on me gradually from one to the other. I had to start taking over things gradually before they died. I had power of attorney, and we had this lady lawyer who arranged that. I had to look after the things. . . . I have never been away from my parents until then. I have always been with them. And, my life changed when they died, because I had to go out and do things and make friends.

Women who made a home with their parents were interdependent in other careers, as well. The woman below was a surrogate parent to her younger siblings and substituted for her mother in other roles. Their relationship changed over the years, with periods of dependence and independence within the mother-daughter relationship. Her mother was "domineering and bossy," an observation she made with a smile:

You know that is what happens when a mother has a daughter home who isn't married. She treats her like a little kid. You'd be surprised. My mother did with me. Oh, my mother wouldn't live without me. She wouldn't want to stay with anyone else. My mother treated me like a 2-year-old. I think because I was with her, my mother could twist me around her finger. And she knew it, and I knew it. Even when we disagreed, I would still do whatever she said. Isn't that something!

She supported her mother financially for about 10 years, until she became ill herself and quit her job. Then, the support she provided for her mother shifted to physical care. She was at home when her mother died. She was grateful that her mother died peacefully at age 85:

I was glad because she went into a coma and didn't suffer. It was a nice death. I think she was always afraid of being an invalid.

This woman was more tolerant of the arrangement she and her mother had worked out; it was her choice to be so involved in her mother's life. She was one of the few never-married women who discussed having intimate relationships with men. She perceived her life as one of conscious choices—not to marry, to delay employment while caring for younger siblings, to enter work after the younger siblings were grown, to quit her job, and to nurse her mother in her old age. She perceived the bargain she struck with her mother to be her natural place, and she perceived her life as very rewarding.

Another never-married woman continued to live with her 92 year old mother. Like many adult child/aging parent pairs, their relationship changed over the years. This woman's income was needed to buy a home for her family during the Depression, and for the past 10 years, she and her mother have become companions, living on her retirement. When they moved recently, she selected the carpeting and draperies because both mother and daughter now consider that the daughter is "the boss." As with the only child above, independence and adult status were conferred on her after age 60. Her comments about not realizing she was grown up were common. Many described how they felt treated as a child by their parents, or they felt like a child themselves:

> Until I was over 60, I regarded her opinions more than now. All at once I realized I was grown up, too. This wasn't because she told me what to do particularly, it was just we knew what she was thinking about you.

In contrast to the tolerance expressed by the 6 women above, 2 other women felt stuck with their parents, and they resented the responsibilities that fell to them. For one woman, there were no other children to care for her parents. She cared for them until she was in her seventies, but she tried as best she could to carve out her own life. In retrospect, she wondered if it was at all worth it because her father never thanked her. Given her heritage and the norms of filial responsibility, she took care of him at her own expense. Caring for her father, who died at age 94, was especially traumatic. She retired from her job because her nursing ability was needed at home, yet her father continued to be domineering and uncooperative until the day he died:

> My life was really rough when I was taking care of my father because they give you a hard time when you are taking care of your own family. . . . After all, you are just a little girl to them.

Finally, one woman expressed ambivalence about caring for her mother. She felt that it was her responsibility to be her mother's caregiver, but she made choices to be independent in terms of work, residence, and companionship. At different intervals in her life, she managed to live apart from her mother, but the passage below reveals the continued emotional interplay of mother and daughter:

> Oh, it was miserable at times. She never treated me like anything but a child. She'd say, "Now aren't you going to put on a sweater, where's your rubbers?" One of my nieces was getting married, and I was getting dressed. It was a stinking, miserable hot day, and I had planned exactly what I was going to wear, and it was so hot that I changed my mind. And in those days, back 23 years ago, you wore gloves if you went to a wedding, and my mother wanted to know where my gloves were. I said, "I don't need mittens." And I said, "If you don't want to let anybody know that you know me, it's perfectly all right with me. Just let me alone."

She lived with her mother most of her life and partially supported her, but she did not provide extensive caregiving until the last 10 years of her mother's life. After 6 years of working full time and providing all the care for her mother, she took a leave of absence from her job. Her brothers and sisters, who were all married, resisted providing relief for her. Carrying the total responsibility was too much after all those years, and she felt forced to put her mother in a nursing home. She expressed resentment about the lack of help she received from her siblings, whose attitude she characterized as follows:

> It's easier for you to take care of her. It's keeping the burden off of us. They didn't ever say that, but that was their idea. You're an old maid. It's your responsibility. When it came to the point where I couldn't take care of her and work, I couldn't retire at that point and have any income comparable to what I'd had, I needed a couple of years. It was just that they couldn't see any reason why I shouldn't be the one to put her in a nursing home, so who do you think made the decision?

When her mother died, she felt relieved that she had received good care. The ambivalence she felt for her mother and her siblings was evident.

Widows and Their Parents

For the most part, the widows concentrated on their own husbands and children after their marital careers began. Eleven widows lost both parents by age 50, but only 3 of these women took care of their parents before they died. For these 3, family of orientation responsibilities continued to middle age. Thus, parent caring was not a lifelong family subcareer for widows in this sample as it was for never-married women (Brody, 1985). One woman delayed marriage to care for her mother during her illness. After this woman married, her mother lived with her until she died 2 years later. This woman was childless during that time, and then adopted a daughter after her mother's death. A second woman was an only child, and there was no one else to take on the caregiving role. She married when she was 30. A third woman lived in her parents' home along with her husband and two sons until her parents died. At that time, she was 44. She married later and was more characteristic of the never-married women in terms of her relationship with her parents:

> I felt awful bad when my husband died, and then I felt worse because my mother died, and I think I felt worse to lose my mother because it is my own blood. And it was very sad for me when I lost my father. I took care of both my parents. My father, too.

The only widow with lifelong caregiving responsibilities for her parents was married at 18 and widowed 25 years later. She helped her mother before she married by caring for her siblings. During her marriage, she had a reprieve from extended family responsibilities. During mid-life, she opened her home to her mother-in-law and father-in-law. Then, in her later years, she took care of her parents before they died. Since her parents were divorced, these were two separate responsibilities. Her experience was atypical of the other women because she cared for both parents and in-laws. Other women had long-term caregiving responsibilities for one or two parents, at most. She lost her mother in 1975, and her father 7 years later:

> I tried having him live with me for awhile, because he was old, but he was very unhappy and he didn't like it at my house, so he went back to his old neighborhood, and he lived there for 17 years until he died. So, I used to cook things, and make rice pudding or bread pudding, or scalloped potatoes and stuff, and take it up to him. He did his own cooking and he did very well, he took his laundry to the laundromat, and he drove his car right up until 6 months before he died. He was a

real rugged big man, and he remembered things that I couldn't remember. He never lost his memory of anything, which my mother
did. The last year of her life, she became quite senile, and I took care
of her most of that year.

This woman was already a widow when her parents needed her late
in life. Her husband was an alcoholic, and they lived separately for a
while. She had established an independence from her parents early
on and then from her husband, so when her parents became dependent upon her in later middle age, she accepted the parent care role
as an extension of her caregiving career (Brody, 1985). Like the
other 3 widows who cared for their aging parents, she noted that
there was no one else to take on the responsibilities of such care.

MARITAL CAREERS

The diversity in the relationships between aging parent
and adult child was similar to the diversity found across long-term
marital relationships. Like the pathways of never-married women,
there were many variations in the widows' family histories. Differences were evident in age at marriage, age at widowhood, length of
childbearing span, and length of marriage. Yet, they all faced tragedies and crises in the course of being spouses and parents, just as the
never-married women did in the course of their lives. Three types of
marital careers were described by the widows, as shown in Table 6.2.
In the first pattern, 8 women maintained what they considered a
"good marriage." In the second pattern, by the time 3 women were
age 52, their husbands had died, and they became independent of
married life. Finally, 4 women described happy marriages in the beginning, but certain events occurred which soured their relationships. The impact of their life events that occurred during adulthood, in conjunction with their marital careers, are examined below.

Vital Marriages

Eight women described marital relationships that
were central to their lives. Their descriptions of the love and
companionship they shared with their husbands and their abil-

TABLE 6.2   Marital Careers by Timing of Marriage

Type of Marriage	On-Time	Delayed	Total
Vital	6	2	8
Good, not central	2	1	3
Soured	2	2	4
Total	10	5	15

ity to cope with crises reflected Cuber and Harroff's (1965) concept of "vital marriages" and Komarovsky's (1962) finding of couple-centered marriages:

> He wasn't the type that wanted to go out all the while. He never put his coat and hat on and said "I'm going out, I'll be back." Where you saw him, you saw me, where you saw me, you saw him.

> He was a kind, gentle, nice man. At first, we were very much in love, and then we became very close friends, and I would go to him for advice. I miss him so much.

> With my husband, I have a lot of good memories. He suffered. He had cancer. He was a great one for nutrition. He also had a great garden that he loved. . . . But we weren't the gushy gushy type. We were never demonstrative in front of people, but we had a lot of respect for each other, and I know with him, too, it was a once in a lifetime deal. I'm sure that if I had gone ahead of him, I don't think that he ever would have married again either. . . . He was a very considerate person, and he was right there to help anybody and if I was sick, he would take right over for me. He could do everything for me. He also was a good electrician and a good plumber, and these were all things that he taught himself.

> I have liked every hour, every week, every month, every year of my marriage. I've loved it all. There are so many memories, that they could more than fill a book, in pictures or in words. I think of myself as being compared to Mrs. Eisenhower, her life was very much the same . . . or the Trumans . . . he was my husband's favorite president, because he was a hell-blowing, ranting kind of a president, but he really meant business, and he was always in love with his wife. They have some of the sweetest moments of his life with her in a book that I read. It tells of how they understood each other so well, that when they were in a room together, they were completely silent, but they would hold hands and knew what the other one was thinking.

In addition to the experiences noted above, other widows described major crises in their lives and how they coped because of the type of relationship they had with their husbands. A week before her son was married, one woman's daughter-in-law had a tragic accident:

> I think that a lot of people go to pieces when things like that happen to them. I think it was my husband that I had to lean on. He was strong. And I think it's really him that pulled us all through that. The way he sat down and talked to my son, I could tell. . . . He was a good husband to me and a good father to the kids. Very thoughtful. . . . He was always putting me first. Then if there's anything left, the children come. I always was putting him ahead of the kids, too. I figure you should for a good marriage. . . . They were good years, and I would do them all over again with the same man.

Another woman spent 49 years with a husband she described as a dreamer. They moved over 50 times during their marriage, and her two sons begged her to divorce him. She said he was selfish because he would quit his job, sell the house and not even consult her. Yet, she said he came first in her life, and she had no regrets:

> When I got married, I married him for keeps. And I loved him so much that I could never love another guy. Never. So, he had his— what should I say—he was a very determined person, and I was easy going. That was partly my fault. I'm sure it was. For putting up with what I did.

One woman spoke of many disappointments and tragedies in her life, which included her father's suicide and her children's divorces. A change of life daughter became pregnant at 17 and had to get married. These personal tragedies were still unresolved for her, but she spoke of her married life in positive terms:

> Well, now that I'm older and I see other marriages and the way they are, we always did things together. I know a lot of them, the husbands could go one way, but when it came to entertainment or anything like that, or if we had anything to do, it was together. Now, as I look back at a lot of them, they didn't go out with one another. But, he and I did do the important things together all the time, and make decisions on everything.

Finally, one woman stated she had a very "romantic" relationship with her husband because they always put each other first:

> Thursdays were paydays, and every Thursday he brought me a red rose, except the first week that daffodils would come out and that was the first sign of spring. So, when I go to the cemetery, I don't bring a lot of plants, I bring one red rose to him.

After 15 years of marriage, her husband was confined to a wheelchair for the remaining 22 years of his life. She went to work, and considered herself lucky to have had her husband as long as she did:

> See, I was very lucky. I had a lot of freedom, and I have been asked since why wouldn't I ever remarry. Because I could never find another man like him. No other man would ever put up with me, because I couldn't have the freedom I had.

Good, but not Central Marriages

Three women who were married less than 30 years and lost their husbands by age 52 noted that they had had good relationships with their husbands, but they rarely think of them now. These women were widowed 22 years ago. During the in-depth interviews, their husbands were rarely mentioned. When asked about this fact, they stated:

> No, I didn't mention my husband, ah, let's see, what can I say about him? He was a real nice guy. He was an ice cream man. He wasn't that important to me, because he hasn't been with me that long.

> Well, he's been gone 22 years. He has been out of my life so long.

> Ah, he was very important to me, I loved him dearly . . . but my children just seemed to come first.

The events these women described were more in terms of their own individual lives. Two of them had histories of illnesses, operations, accidents, and near-death experiences. They had large families and many descendants who occupied their time and energy before and after their husbands died. As one woman noted:

My children were more important than my marriage. The important
thing with being married and having children is to let your children be
first and to let your husband think he is. That is my philosophy! My
husband never knew the kids were first, but I wonder. That last year
he lived, he said to me, "It's so funny, we have been together all these
years, but I never was first with you." And I said, "What do you mean,
you never were first with me?" He said, "You always put God first." I
said, "Well, He is supposed to be first." And that was the end of that
conversation.

Soured Relationships

Four women described their marriages as happy at first,
but over the years, their relationships soured. They said their husbands changed, and their relationships ended before they became
widows. Yet, all 4 women continued to live with their husbands, and
they took care of them until they died, perceiving few alternatives,
as Acker et al. (1981), Bernard (1972), and Rubin (1976, 1983)
found in their studies of women's disappointments about the gap
between the ideology and the reality of marriage. The widow who
cared for her parents and in-laws said the last 10 years of marriage
was her low point in life.

Well, if I want to be honest with you, our marriage was kinda rocky.
My husband wasn't home a lot. He would be gone, so I learned to become very independent. He was an alcoholic—let's be frank. He
would just disappear for 4 or 5 days. Life wasn't very easy for me at
that time. . . . I thought more than once of leaving, but his family was
very supportive of me and helped me a great deal. One time I had my
car all packed and was ready to take off, and I thought, "What kind
of a deal is this, they're his kids. How are you going to feed them?",
so I stayed.

A second woman described the first 18 years of marriage as "perfect," until her husband changed. She filed for a divorce, but her
lawyer convinced her to stay:

I really could write a book. He just went completely haywire again, so
by the time I got him back after 5 years, I finally hammered into his
head about getting drunk, so then he didn't get drunk anymore. But, I
figured this going out every night, it was something he had to do. I

mean I never nagged about it. I never said much about it, because I thought he was old enough to know what he was doing wrong. I think, my way of analyzing it, it made him feel important, in going with all these dizzy women, it wasn't anything that I didn't do, because I was always there, for like sex, or whatever, it amazed me, he was a very nice guy, but by the time he died, he was nothing but a dirty old barfly. I hate to say that, because I can't believe what he did. He wanted to make everybody. . . . So, the lawyer said, I must have been 55 then, "I don't think you should get a divorce because who's going to support you at your age?", and he said I better just put up with it. So, I just put up with it.

Another woman was the only widow who said she regretted getting married and having children. Although she was married for 45 years, she wished she had her life to live over again. She described many instances when her husband "humiliated" her, and she felt she was a failure as a mother because her children divorced. She said having a disabled child was the cause of her marital breakdown:

> After I really got to know him, he was not the person I thought he was. We could not sit down and communicate. I don't think he ever forgave me for putting our son in the state institution.

Finally, one woman described a rocky marriage that endured for 40 years. After they were married a year, he was involved in a robbery and went away. They separated once more, and when he came back, she was working. She supported the family for the rest of her married life. Her marriage was bittersweet, as her description of life with a "drinking husband" indicated:

> He couldn't go anyplace. He just sat home and drank. And he couldn't draw any Social Security because he wasn't sick enough, but I was just as pleased because he'd just spend it on drink. . . . I didn't have any regrets because I figure your life is all mapped out for you. . . . So, I worked and came home and watched the television, then go to bed and get up and go to work, and I took 28 years of that. . . . He got mean when he drank, drinking, falling over, wet the bed. But, he was a wonderful person otherwise. Everybody liked him, and no one ever knew he was like that. He was like a Dr. Jekyll and Mr. Hyde.

The ambivalence she felt toward him compared with some of the never-married women's feelings for their mothers. She achieved an early independence in marriage and was the backbone of the family, but she was lonely without her husband.

COMPARISON OF ADULT CHILD/AGING PARENT AND MARITAL CAREERS

The context of caregiving allows the variety of family-keeping roles and family extension roles of women to emerge. Juxtaposing a traditional pathway with a "deviant" one reveals hidden dimensions in women's caregiving. The main adult bond among never-married women and widows was the mother-daughter and the husband-wife relationship, respectively. Although they did not take on the roles of wife and mother, in this study, never-married women were not bereft of family; many were connected to parents by sharing a home and livelihood and being lifelong companions and caregivers, just as married women were connected to husbands. Others, regardless of marital status, felt less connected to kin than those described above. The assumption of characteristics associated with married versus single status distorts the bonds that women establish in adulthood.

The adult child/aging parent career that dominated the middle years of the never-married women was as varied and complex as the classic descriptions of marital relationships. Most single women who were interdependent with their mothers and most widows who were interdependent with their husbands expressed the same type of complex feelings about these relationships. Similarly, there were women in both groups who were less connected emotionally to their parents or husbands, respectively, and who sought, instead, intimacy in relationships with children or friends. Finally, a few women in both groups did not form lasting adult bonds with anyone; their relative isolation may result in their dependence upon welfare institutions in very old age (Brody, 1985; Gubrium, 1976; Hareven, 1982a). The main finding from these data is that women did not need to be a wife or mother to be connected to family in essential, lifelong ways. Intimacy and mutuality did not occur just in marriage or with one's own children. As studies of marriage have found, a married woman's most intimate friend is often not her husband (Bernard, 1972; Rubin, 1976, 1983). Parents, siblings, nieces and nephews can be just as important in the lives of single women.

TAKING CARE OF CHILDREN

In a third type of caregiving relationship, children were very central to these women. Those who had their own children and grandchildren recounted the events in their parental subcareers that were most meaningful to them. The never-married women, as well, performed a variety of family-keeping roles in relation to children, as shown in Table 6.3.

Never-Married Women and Their Children

Fourteen never-married women described the relationships they had with children throughout their lives. The only woman who did not take care of children was an only child who remained childish herself until her parents died. However, she described her pet as the only member of her family left alive. She plans to stay in her home rather than move to an apartment so it will have a place to live.

The major role that women described was taking care of their brothers' and sisters' children. Thirteen never-married women had nieces or nephews. Ten of these women performed the role of "surrogate mother." Three women did not have a central role in raising the children, but they spoke fondly of them, caring at a distance. They noted the children's accomplishments and specific dates such as when they were born. A typical response in this category was this description of a brother's children:

> His oldest girl is married, and his oldest boy is doing research work at some university. And one of them is a veterinarian's assistant. And another girl is just starting college, and I don't know what she is majoring in. The boys, I think are in math and doing research work. I guess they are all kinda smart!

The 10 women who served as surrogate mothers were involved in their nieces' and nephews' upbringing, and the relationships continued to the present time. They provided financial assistance to send a child to college. They bought them clothes, and babysat over the weekend so the parents could take a trip. These 10 women expressed

TABLE 6.3 Never-Married Women's Involvement with Children

Type of Relationship		Total
Distant or no involvement:		4
I stayed childish myself	1	
caring but distant aunt	3	
Lifelong involvement:		11
baby nurse only, no nieces or nephews	1	
surrogate mother to siblings' children	4	
surrogate mother and professional childcare role	6	
Total		15

pride in their role as surrogate mothers. Typical experiences of surrogate mothering were:

> I love my nephew, and I just worship the ground that he walks on. I love that boy. When he went to get his Baptism certificate to get married, he said that "My aunt was like a mother to me and was better than my mother, instead of just an aunt." He said, "My aunt never refused me a thing all the while I was growing up."

> I believe I was born for a certain purpose here on earth. . . . My purpose has been to take care of all these kids that have come along. Of course, they call me their second mother. I'm not as close as they would have been to their real mother, but I take care of those kids. . . . If my sister wanted to go out someplace, she just called me and I'd usually go. Sometimes, she'd go out of town for the weekend, and I'd stay with them. Probably they didn't obey me the way they would her, but what difference does it make. I think that's why I get along so well with them now, because we grew up together. But, they're the only relatives I have now, so I have to get along with them.

> One of my nephews, well, he's my little honey. You oughta see the article he wrote in the Catholic newspaper. Beautiful!

> Now, my niece right there is so cute. She'll say to me, "When I was young, I thought I had two mothers." She had me and her own mother, because I was so close to the family.

> We have always been very close to my brother's kids. In fact, I tell them what to do without thinking twice about it. They have all expressed their feeling that some of their life was different because they spent so much time with us.

Many of the women who functioned as surrogate mothers moved into the family position of matriarch after their sisters died. Like their widowed peers, they became the head of the family. Mainly, this was a later life experience, but it was rooted in the relationship with children that they established during their middle years. For example, one never-married woman referred to her sister's descendants as "my kids":

> My sister had 4 kids and 13 grandchildren. Since she died, I'm the matriarch of the family. They all come to me, and I'm pretty lucky to have them.

Finally, 7 never-married women had "professional" child care roles. Three of these women were employed for at least 10 years as live-in housekeepers. Their duties included taking care of the children in the house. One woman remembered the experience with fondness, and she indicated just how important she felt her role was:

> They have two boys, the older one is a doctor now himself. The last time I saw him, he was in the department store, and he had a little girl with him, and I was going down on the escalator, and he was coming around to go to the shoe department. So, he says hello to me, and I said, "Hello there!" So he says to the little girl that "she used to take care of me when I was a little boy."

The other 4 women interacted with babies, children, and young people in more professional roles. One woman said the young salesmen at the company where she worked referred to her as "their mother." Another woman was an elementary schoolteacher for 42 years. Two women were "baby nurses" for over 20 years. They lived in the family's home, provided child care, and taught new mothers about taking care of infants. Both women still received cards and pictures from the children and mothers for whom they cared. One woman attended the wedding of a child she had taken care of 30 years before, and she described how exciting it was to see her "babies" once again:

> I had a wonderful time. Seeing these five children, actually nine of my babies that night, you can imagine how I felt. They were all family. Two sisters, one had five and one had four. So it was really fun. They

were just as excited as I was. I couldn't believe it. They said I was still wearing the same earrings, and I had an accordion back then, and I used to take it with me, and the kids asked me if I still had my accordion. It was the highlight of the winter. Just that one evening—to see those kids again.

Widows and Their Children

The widows described their children, grandchildren, and great-grandchildren in terms of "how they turned out." With few exceptions, they were proud of their children, as 2 women indicated:

> My kids, they are great. They are awful good to me. They are always calling me and checking on me. They all turned out good.

> My older daughter is fabulous. She had the highest IQ in the schools and the teachers loved her. She's always been a leader.

They expressed disappointments if their children divorced, and 2 women blamed themselves for failing as a mother in such cases. However, other women blamed their children's spouses for causing the divorce. Three women had children who died, and these were very traumatic events in their lives.

Several women described how they felt when their children married and left home. They regretted when their last child left, possibly because they were widowed earlier in life and faced an empty home alone:

> Of course, every time one of my children left home and got married, it was an adjustment. And the last one, when he left, that was the biggest adjustment of all because then I was *really* alone.

Two women noted that it was their *husbands* who cried when their children married:

> He was pretty devoted to his family. As each one got married, he took it so hard. I didn't because I was with them from the time they were born until they left.

> He never wanted them to marry. He loved them too much. After my son married, he broke down and sobbed. And, I said he made me feel inadequate because we had been married all that time.

The 2 women with the most children had the least contact with them in comparison to women who had between one and five children. Both these women were widowed at age 52 and were in poor health. They wanted to live with their children, but no one wanted them.

There were 8 women who were independent and healthy, and they appeared to be the most satisfied with their children. Like never-married women who performed surrogate-mothering roles, these widows had the best of both worlds. "Not being a burden to my children" was a common theme, characteristic of older adults in general (Brody, 1985; Shanas, 1979), as one woman noted:

> A lot of people think you're old and your life is finished, but it isn't. You know, in one way it's one of the best times of our life, for the simple reason we have a nice apartment and we can live on our Social Security. We don't have to go to our children and ask for handouts, so our pride, dignity, and independence has not been taken away from us. I always want to be independent. And if the day comes that I can't take care of myself, I'm going to sign myself into a nursing home, because I don't think my children should be burdened with me. I don't believe in that.

Thus, "intimacy at a distance" characterized the current relationships 8 women had with their descendants, as Neugarten and Weinstein (1964) found in their study of grandparenting styles. They valued this type of relationship because it allowed them to live independently but still have an emotional relationship with descendants (Shanas, 1979).

Their relationships with grandchildren and great-grandchildren were similar to the "surrogate mother" and "fond but distant aunt" roles of the never-married women. Nine widows were actively involved in their descendants' lives. They babysat, played games, took them on trips, and bought them toys and clothes. Their grandchildren were a source of pleasure and assistance:

> I share my time with my grandchildren, too. I have them over for dinner sometimes, or I will go over there sometimes, too. I let the children come here for the weekends, and they stay overnight. They just love it.

> My grandson is the most important person to me. It used to be my

son, but he moved away, so his son has taken his place for me. . . . He comes to visit me. He does all these little things for me. He put shelves in my closet, and he took care of my car the other day, it needed new brake shoes; they wanted $200, and he took care of it. . . . I always had a chest of drawers in my breakfast room, and in the bottom one it was full of toys for all the kids, and they loved it. And he has always been very close, I guess. We just get along so well. I have one other grandson like that. It's not that you love one any more than the other, it's just the personality.

The other 6 women did not have the same opportunities to participate in the daily lives of grandchildren and great-grandchildren, perhaps because most of them did not live in the same geographical area. Yet, they were proud of their accomplishments in much the same way as never-married aunts were.

SUMMARY

All of the women in this study were caregivers. Never-married women and widows alike played important roles in the lives of children. Regarding adult relationships, widows were involved primarily with a husband; never-married women were involved primarily with a parent. In terms of the adult child/aging parent subcareer, never-married women provided insight about the mother-daughter relationship from the perspective of the daughter, and widows provided insight about the mother-daughter relationship from the perspective of the mother. As the women entered old age, many assumed the position of family matriarch. While widows noted the ambivalence they felt as mothers in their position as head of the family, lifelong single women expressed that they had most of the rewards and few of the problems associated with biological mothering. Being an aunt was an essential role for never-married women, but not for widows. Widows occupied the important family positions of wife, mother, grandmother, and great-grandmother. Never-married women occupied the important family positions of parent caregiver, lifelong companion, surrogate mother, and aunt.

These data help reveal hidden subcareers of the family life course for women from the 1910 birth cohort. Although much of the contemporary parent caregiving literature focuses on the married middle aged daughter as caregiver (see also Finch & Groves, 1983; Troll, 1986), in the present study, parent care was primarily the domain of never-married women. Since their birth in the early 20th century, the life course has lengthened, the birth rate has fallen, and family size has decreased in subsequent decades (Uhlenberg, 1980), requiring a variety of kin (i.e., married, unmarried, male, female) and welfare institutions to be enlisted as caregivers today (Brody, 1985; Wright, 1983). In this study, the family-keeping roles of never-married women are rooted in their gender, class, cohort, and individual and family life course decisions, correlates that are associated with the structurally essential role of spinster found throughout history (Chambers-Schiller, 1984; Dixon, 1978; Watkins, 1984). Their family-keeping roles are part of women's historic caregiving careers.

7

Growing Old as Single Women

In childhood, young adulthood, and middle age, the women in the study experienced enduring cohort effects as daughters of working-class families. Their life course careers—friendship, work, residential, and health—were organized around family subcareers. Marital and parental status differentiated their lives in adulthood in obvious ways. Now, in old age, their lives converged again as both widows and never-married women were single and headed their own households. The ways in which they described their lives did not follow a clear-cut progression of orderly stages. They wove the past into their descriptions of the present. The women's current status and perceptions about their life course variations are examined below by comparing their perceptions of being single in old age, their life review assessments, and their views of family subcareers within the context of marriage norms.

BEING ALONE

Most of the women were able to maintain their independence by relying on at least one other resource. The size and structure of their support networks varied, and the women were adept at resource pooling to compensate for deficits, either in the kin and friendship networks or the social services that were available to them. As Shanas (1979) reported, old people prefer to maintain some physical distance from kin without being isolated from them. For example, the children of a woman with hearing and visual problems provided transportation and shopping which enabled her to maintain her independence at home. A smaller number of women, however, appeared to be in a time of transition, where they questioned their present security and revealed their worries about the future. Although these women had established support networks for their later years, changes were occurring that threatened their security. Being single in old age is a common experience for women, as Glick (1979) found in his study of women 65 and older: 36.5% were still married, and 63.5% were widowed, never-married, or divorced. The key issue the women struggled with was the threat of becoming dependent. Old age is an especially vulnerable time when multiple losses can render a person dependent upon others. They were cognizant of their vulnerability, having endured since childhood various threats to their security.

Implications for Widows

The transition to being single occurred when the people with whom they lived in middle age died, moved away, or became unavailable. The meaning of the transition to being alone in old age varied, for the most part, due to the context of their previous transitions, rather than to marital status. The majority of the women who lived alone spoke positively about their transition to independence as old women, as reflected in the words of one widow:

> But now, this is my life. I had to organize my life and adjust my life for myself. Before, I had him, and we were both involved and did different things. We were always together. . . . I think I am more independent than I was before when my husband was living. I am very independent now and can manage pretty well. I am getting along pretty good.

All 15 widows lived alone, and most of them had the opportunity to be with family at their own discretion. They described their current lifestyle as a time of freedom from family and work responsibilities. It was the *option* to move to her own apartment and have access to kin on her own terms that seemed to be the ideal situation for the following woman, who was typical of the widows:

Living here is the easiest, nicest thing that's ever happened to me because before, I had a lot of responsibility, and today I don't have responsibilities at all.

Several widows said that they did not want to remarry because they were afraid of an older man getting sick, and then they would have to take care of him. These women had passed through one transition to widowhood and did not want to tackle a new marriage. The following quotes are from 3 women who had a vital, good but not central, or sour marriage, respectively:

I have my own life now . . . and I could never get another man like my husband. I feel that I've had a good life, and history never repeats itself as to that part.

I didn't want to be tied down. I was having too good of a time alone. When men are older, they want you near them every minute. You can't move! And that is not for me. No! Never. When I had been independent all these years, and here is somebody I could marry, but not if I had to stay home. Now, I could see it if he had a lot of money, and we could go away on trips all the time. I could see that, but not being tied down at home. Suppose he gets sick. Then, you have to take care of him, and I couldn't see that either. So, I am better off the way I am.

I never had any desire to remarry. People use to ask me why I never remarry and I said, "if I could find someone to take as good of care of me as I take care of myself, maybe I would consider it."

The process of accepting one's own aging is evident in the following widow's comment:

Now, this is old age, and I told the doctor the other day, I don't want to accept it, but he said, "You gotta. You're lucky you're getting older instead of the other way." So, I figure you gotta accept it. You gotta think the next phase is going to be better than the last, and so it is . . . because if things aren't alright now, you can always look to something better in the future.

Nine widows prepared for the transition to old age by building a support network over time. They were active in senior citizen organizations and with friends, they lived independently, they had adequate transportation, and their health was not a problem. In contrast, an additional 4 widows were in transition for various reasons.

These women accepted their old age, but there was a danger in their current circumstances that could render them dependent in the near future. Two had only one living child who did not live near them. They worried that if their health failed any more, they were only one step away from dependency, and they were not yet prepared for that. Two other widows were both strongly engaged in kin networks, but their responses to current patterns revealed other variations. One of these women still grieved for her husband who had died 7 years before. The other woman's health was failing, but she relied on her children for support, and her outlook was positive.

Finally, 2 widows did not perceive that their children or other relatives were available to them. In spite of a large number of actual kin living in the area, both women felt alone, and they were much more negative about the future. Their life histories were dominated by tragedies, and their past experiences continued to burden them. Unlike most of the widows, both women had unresolved feelings of bitterness about their parents, siblings, and children. One had an unhappy marriage, and the other became a widow over 20 years before.

Implications for Never-Married Women

Never-married women, as well, primarily lived alone, but there was a great deal of variation in what their solitary status meant for them. They tended to replace the loss of parents with friends or other members of their families. Only 4 women in the study, all never-married, shared a residence with another person. One lived with her sister, and a second lived with her mother. A third lived with her boyfriend, but he was in the hospital and not likely to return. The brother of a fourth woman stayed with her for extended visits.

Like the widows, the never-married women anticipated that growing older meant living alone, as the following woman noted:

I am not a widow, but I'm the same as a widow. I'm a woman living alone, going home to an empty house, and you know a lot of people will invite me some place, and I just have to say no, because I don't come home alone to an empty house, and that is the way it should be. Now, if I go out to places with the senior citizens, either my friend or his wife both will follow me home. And if it is the case of leaving when it is dark, he will come over and get me. That is one of the ways that they help me. I don't have to worry about going home after dark.

Just as there were 9 widows who had made adequate provisions for their old age, there were also 9 never-married women in similar situations. The majority of these 9 never-married women have always been independent, and they managed to function on their own within an interdependent network of siblings and their offspring, friends, and social services. They arrived at their current status in various ways, but they were pleased with their living arrangement and the provisions they had made for themselves.

Four never-married women were potentially vulnerable. Two of these 4 women were in transition. Both were suffering from chronic physical problems that were compounded by a loss. One woman had just lost her closest companion, whom she did not expect to return from the hospital. The other woman had renewed an old feud with her sister, and she worried that it would alter her relationship with her sister's daughter. These losses threatened the women's independence.

Two of these never-married women were not in transition, but they worried about having very small support networks. Both women had few remaining kin living near them, and they relied on friends and senior center employees for support. One woman, for example, lost her mother 20 years ago, and her only living relatives, a nephew and his family, live in a distant part of the state. For now, she feels she is in a safe environment, with friends and services available to her, but she worries about the future. Although she described her relationship with her family as "good," she was not quite ready to accept a position as an outsider in their home:

> I wouldn't interfere with what they are doing. I don't know if I want to live with somebody all the time. I have been alone for a long time, and of course, I never had any sisters, so I was practically alone anyways all my life.

Finally, 2 women were in danger of becoming truly isolated. For one, there were many people in her network, but she had unresolved relationships with most of them:

I used to think I was good, but now I think I'm horrible ... now that I am old, there's nobody around. You'd got to be horrible or there would be somebody.

The other woman found herself alone in the last few years after her father's death. She had spent most of later adulthood in relative isolation from others while she cared for him. Trying to establish new ties was a slow process and not always rewarding. Her words suggest her sadness of being alone:

Sometimes, my friends will call to see if I'm alright, and I'll say, "Yes, but I haven't talked to anybody all day." Sometimes a whole day goes by and I won't talk to anyone, and you can get very alone if you let yourself. You can get very sorry for yourself.

LIVES IN REVIEW: THE TYPE OF LIFE I HAVE LED

In the process of recounting their life events, the women placed their lives in perspective. The in-depth interviews allowed the women to share their insights, perceptions, and fears about their lives over time. Life review (Butler, 1968) is a guided self-evaluation process based on Erikson's (1963) last stage of integrity versus despair. Reflecting on the past enables the meaning of old age to be described in relation to the whole of life (Runyan, 1984). The women's comments concerned whether they thought their lives were dull, hard, or full. More of the never-married women perceived that their lives had been dull and fewer perceived that their lives had been full, as shown in Table 7.1. Never-married women and widows alike had trouble perceiving the fullness and value in the lives of single women. As discussed above, marital status did not differentiate their transition to old age, but their perceptions of life course typicality did distinguish the never-married from the widowed.

"I've Had a Dull Life"

There were 9 women who noted that they had a "dull, uneventful life." Seven were never-married and only 2 were widowed. Typical responses from the never-married were as follows:

TABLE 7.1   Life Review Perceptions: The Type of Life I Have Led

	A Dull Life	A Hard Life	A Full Life	Total
Never-married	7	4	4	15
Widowed	2	4	9	15
Total	9	8	13	30

Mine is an everyday, same kind of life . . . just one big blah! I don't think I ever did anything out of the ordinary. I didn't amount to anything when I was young.

Not much happened to me. I led a dull life.

Well, there's nothing to elaborate on. I told you I wasn't going to be your most interesting subject. Everything has always gone along on an even keel. As I say, I had the same position all my life, had the same friends all my life. . . . Maybe I've led an uneventful life, but I've been happy in the life I've led.

The 2 widows described their lives in similar terms:

I don't have too much of a life. I think a lot of people have had a nicer life than I had, but I accept it. I'm a very plain person.

My life wasn't filled with many events, actually. They don't boil down to too much.

"I've Had a Hard Life"

There were 4 never-married women and 4 widows who described their lives as full of hard times and hard work. Three of these women were more accepting than the others because they never expected anything more from life than hardship. They were grateful to have their own apartment or home in their later years; life was an uphill climb, and finally, in old age, they had some comfort. The woman who lived with a domineering father was still hopeful that the future would bring something positive, though at other times, she had been doubtful:

My life has been one adjustment after another. . . . We all have our ups and downs. I just feel that some of your downs are some of the things that make you strong.

Five other women described their lives in terms of hard times, and they had strong regrets about their lives, as in the case of the widow who regretted marrying, having children, and not going to college. Another never-married woman, who had previously revealed herself to be a fighter, expressed regret about her accident in childhood:

I believe that why did I have to live this kinda life? Why? I was only 3 years old, what did I do then? Nothing! I was just a baby. I could picture if it happened when I was grown up, maybe there'd be a reason, but at 3, I can't see it. . . . I think of all the things I missed in life that I could've enjoyed, like dancing, skiing, skating, all those sports, I would've loved them, and I always wanted to be a nurse.

"I've Had a Full Life"

Finally, 13 women in the sample, 9 of whom were widows, stated that they had led full or exciting lives. The widowed group felt their lives were full because they had experienced the normative life course involving the stages of marriage and motherhood. If they were able to travel, to live in different cities, to have friends and to maintain their health, they perceived their lives as even fuller. Typical comments from widows were:

I feel like I've had everything in life that is possible to have. And I feel real happy about that, and I feel real good about it. And I figure I did my utmost, and I'm happy, and what else is there to think about?

I have had more different ways that things have happened than most people. My life has been pretty diversified, you know. I have done a lot of things.

My life was like a rough night at sea. It's ups and downs. When I reminisce sometimes, I think about what I might have changed in my life, and I don't think I would have changed anything, except I'd have my husband back with me, but that's not to be.

The 4 never-married women, on the other hand, felt their lives were full because they were *unlike* other never-married women.

They noted they had exciting jobs, had traveled to Europe, and had strong friendships and family relationships. As one woman described:

> I know there are single women who aren't as happy as I am, because they haven't had the activities and the connections that I had. Now, I worked for a big company, and I was very close to all these agents, and I was with their wives, and they never had parties without me. And that was my way of life. Where, others, like there were girls that I worked with who were never invited to anything . . . and I've had it a lot better than married girls. I've gone with a girl who called me this morning, and I remember when she was young, and she had to ask her husband to give her a little change. And that used to burn me up, that she had no money, so I would pay the checks for a lot of married women, whom I wouldn't change places with for love, money or marbles.

PERCEPTIONS OF MARITAL STATUS: NORMATIVE, DEVIANT, OR VARIANT?

The perceptions of the never-married women who felt they had led uneventful lives seem inconsistent with the tragedies, crises, and accomplishments they recounted throughout their lives. Their experiences were as diverse as the widows, yet the "fullness" of their own lives seemed invisible to most of them. On the other hand, widows perceived that they had led eventful and typical lives. They expected to marry, and motherhood was unquestionably tied to being wives. The focus of their recollections was mostly of middle and later life events in their marital careers, a distinctly different view from how the never-married women characterized their lives. The never-married women focused upon their families of orientation and their young adult years. Events and transitions occurred in their lives which limited their opportunities to marry. Very few offered accounts or explanations (Scott & Lyman, 1968) for their non-married status. Although they had come to terms with being single, they regretted not having children. Still, they cared for aging parents and were second mothers to the children in their lives.

The traditional female life course is normative, socialized, and supported by the ideology of compulsory marriage and motherhood (Bernard, 1972; 1981a; Chodorow & Contratto, 1982; Rich, 1980; Rubin, 1983). The widows in this study had an insider's point of view about this expected lifestyle. As will be shown below, the widows considered their lives to be "normal," and they were puzzled by questions asking them to compare their life course to women who never married. They perceived never-married women as outsiders. Most said they knew only married people, and those who knew never-married women referred to them stereotypically as old maids.

The never-married women shared this insider-outsider perspective. They did not identify with other lifelong singles. Their points of reference were the traditional female life course, i.e., "I'm am not a widow, but I am the same as a widow," and their own exceptionality in relation to other never-married women, i.e., the never-married woman who lived with her mother and later shared an apartment with her brother. She felt her life was different from other never-married women and more like married women's lives:

> My life was different because of the fact of having been so closely associated with my brother. That made a difference there. That filled the gap. Well, we were close, and I would have him to turn to in case of emergency. So others didn't have that.

Perceptions of Being Never-Married

The women were asked to discuss whether or not they thought it made a difference in a person's life if she married and had children. They were also asked to describe how they thought they were similar to or different from other never-married women as well as women who were married, had children, and were now widows. With few exceptions, they stated that their lives were different from their widowed counterparts. Also, some of them felt they were "better off" than other never-married women. The way in which they described their own lives in comparison to other women's was in terms of either not wanting to marry or having regrets that they did not. Eight women stated that they had no regrets about not marrying. On the other hand, 7 women had some regrets, primarily because they did not have their own children and felt more alone in old age since many of their lifelong companions had died. Three of these 7 women did not regret remaining single; rather, they missed having their own children. Four of the 7 women expressed deep regrets; they felt their lives would have been better if they had become wives and mothers. The responses of never-married women, as compared to widows, are summarized in Table 7.2.

No regrets. Three themes were evident among the 8 women who accepted their never-married status. First, they stated they never really considered getting married, and they did not regret the life they led. For example:

> Marriage wasn't that important to me, but I used to have girlfriends who would say to me, "You are the first one of our group to have dated, so how come you're not married?" They used to think it was terrible because I'm not married, and I wouldn't ever change places with them. So, I have been very happy with my life. I think it has been fantastic, and I would never want to go back and lead my life again, because if I did, it probably wouldn't have been as good.

Only one woman in this group offered an account for why she did not marry, and yet she explained, "I have never been sorry":

> Well, it has been kind of a lonely life for me to be alone, but I feel like this, I could have been married. I was engaged to be married, and I wouldn't marry no jailbird. His brother was a jailbird. Anybody that would come out and ask for money to get his brother out of jail, that is where I draw the line.

Second, they viewed the life of a married woman with children as different from their own. They were aware of the problematic aspects of marriage, such as alcoholic husbands, tedious housework, and having to answer to a man, having found out beforehand, unlike their more traditional peers, that it was no escape from such problems in the family of orientation (Rapp, 1982; Rubin, 1976):

> Well, my brother-in-law, my sister's husband, used to work in the brewery. Every holiday, he was stone drunk. I saw so much of it, and I made up my mind, I will never get married, and I didn't. I had a very happy life. But it was lonesome at times, I admit it, but after all, that is the kind of life I chose.

> I think I'd have felt very sorry for myself! I think of all the work and the responsibilities. I don't think I could have taken it. . . . No, I just

TABLE 7.2   Comparison of Marital Status Perceptions

NEVER-MARRIED WOMEN

NO REGRETS:
I have come to terms with remaining single, past and present: 8
    I never considered getting married;
    I have never been sorry;
    I have had the best of both worlds.

AMBIVALENCE:
Regrets about not having children, but no regrets about marriage: 3
    I have missed not having my own children, BUT
      —I have been close to my nieces and nephews;
      —I've just become too independent;
      —you never know, you can get a lemon.

REGRETS AND DISAPPOINTMENTS: 4
Regrets about not marrying and not having children:
    Broken engagements.
    Now that I'm alone, I wish I had married and had kids.

		Total:	15

WIDOWS

NO REGRETS ABOUT MARRIAGE AND MOTHERHOOD	11
AT LEAST I HAD CHILDREN	3
I SHOULD NEVER HAVE MARRIED OR HAD CHILDREN	1

	Total:	15

didn't want to get married. Maybe it was because I had enough doing my brother's clothes and laundry. I couldn't have taken another man.

I think if you have a family to worry about, you have a husband you have to send out everyday and he comes back with some money for you at the end of the week, I think there's gotta be a difference. I never regretted I didn't, though, let me add that, I never regretted I didn't.

Third, 6 of the women said that they have had children around them all their lives, but without major parental responsibilities, they had the best of both worlds:

As I say, I used to like my sister's kids and take care of them all the time, but if I were stuck with them all the time, well, as it was, I could go home at night. After being with them all day, I could go home at night. That's where the difference lies.

I've been a lot freer. Some people probably would say that I've missed an awful lot, but I've had an awful lot of what I think is the best part. It's like grandparents, when you can be a surrogate mother, and have exactly the same responsibilities, not the overall lifetime responsibilities, but the kind of day-to-day responsibilities of kids that parents have left in your charge. And you do that with the same kids over a long period of time, I think that you get the best of all worlds. When the kids come, they drive you up the wall, and by gosh, they're going to go home to their own bed, their parents are going to have to buy them shoes and clothes and educate them. I'm so glad to see them and I so love holding the little one, and cuddling them, and I'm so glad when they close that front door.

I didn't miss having my own children. Listen, you don't have to have children of your own to have children! I had brothers and sisters around me all the time. My nieces and nephews, and especially my one nephew have been great. I didn't need my own. A marriage doesn't solve everything in life. No, I didn't need it.

The only never-married woman without surrogate children thought of herself as childish because she spent many years at home with her parents. She never considered getting married or having children:

The thought never crossed my mind. Not a bit. I didn't have anything against men, but maybe I stayed kinda childish for quite a few years. I just wasn't interested in them.

The experiences and perceptions of these 8 women were captured by the teacher, who lived a life of her own choice:

I don't miss being married. You can't miss what you haven't been.

Ambivalence. Three women were sorry that they did not have children, especially as they grew old. They said they did not have the chance to marry because they had to work or take care of their mothers:

That is one thing I really missed. I look back now, and I wished I had, but at the time I was taking care of my mother. It is very difficult bringing your mother in. I love children. I do miss the fact that I never had children, and this is why I've given so much of my love to my nieces and nephews.

Well I didn't have it, but I think that the happiest time in a woman's life is getting married and having children. Of course, some people don't want children. But I love kids. And my nieces' children, I enjoy them very much.... You've got your children then. Sometimes I wished I had gone out and met someone and married and had children, but I always told my mother, I never wanted to be married unless I could have children.

The mothers of both of these women figured prominently in their recollections regarding their missed opportunity to marry. For the first one above, there was never any question that her first responsibility was to care for her mother; finding a way to fit marriage into her family of orientation responsibilities was her consideration. There was also a sense of unrealistic assessment about what marriage would be like. They regretted not having children, rather than not having a husband. They had enough responsibility without adding a husband. Thus, they appeared to romanticize the actual experience of marriage and parenthood. They came to terms with their single status eventually, yet conveyed resignation about their missed opportunity, as another woman expressed it:

I don't think I ever would have wanted to have my own. I was afraid to have children. . . . Maybe it would drive me crazy. I don't know, I just had to make the best of it. I didn't marry, so I had to make the best of it. I know a lot of the men I used to know in school and when I was younger. I see them now, and I always think "I'm glad I didn't marry him" and stuff like that. They change when they get older. They aren't as nice as when they were younger. I've just become too independent.

Although these 3 women felt they missed out on not having their own children, they were engaged in the lives of their nieces and nephews. Ultimately, they felt they were better off than their ever-married counterparts and balanced their regrets with realistic assessments of their lifelong single status:

Maybe I'm a little happier. I never had to contend with, you know, you can never tell what you're getting. You can get a lemon.

Well, I always had good times, and I always enjoyed myself, and I always said I could go where I wanted to go. I was never tied down. You didn't have a boss there telling you you couldn't go. You know what it would be like.

Only one of the 15 women described how she felt out of place in the company of married women. Her regret about her status was indicated in her description of the difference between the two life courses:

Well, as I say, when a girl gets married, her life changes, and you aren't as close to her as you used to be. . . . You just don't fit in with their life. . . . I just think their life is different, because I would go to my girlfriend's house, and I would just feel out of place when their husband was there and you don't have a man with you. Things were different. I don't know what it was, but it just wasn't the same. . . . Well, they got their husband, and they probably got their children, and they probably don't want to bother with an old maid.

Regrets and disappointments. The remaining 4 never-married women openly acknowledged their regret and disappointment about staying single. As 2 women who never mentioned having a relationship with a man indicated, they felt their lives would have been fuller with a husband and children:

You'd have more places to go with your husband and have somebody to talk to and have fun with now and then, you know, instead of being in the house all the time by yourself. I always thought my sister had a pretty good life with her husband, because he was a farmer, and he used to take the kids, like in the fall, they'd go and gather nuts and they worked. He didn't have a real garden, but he worked on a farm so that he had garden produce.

Well, I kind of wish that I had gotten married, because I would have enjoyed my own children and grandchildren. I kind of wish that I had gotten married instead of being single. Yeah, I would have been a good mother and had a good home. I don't know how many kids I would have had, but I would have had my kids anyways.

The 2 women who had broken engagements also mentioned their regrets about missed opportunities:

> But I find now that I think of him more than before because I'm not as busy now. It seems like I think of him more the last few years. I have been thinking of what we could have had. He was the kind of fella we would have aged along together. He liked doing things that I liked. He was an only child; we did a lot of things with his family, and I think we would have had a nice life together. That's awfully young to be killed.

> Your life would be fuller if you had children, especially if you loved kids. I always loved kids. That was my one disappointment in life, not having a baby. My boyfriend always says, "I shoulda given you a baby," and I say, "yeah, you should have."

Both women balanced their regrets and unfulfilled experiences with their pride in what they had managed to accomplish in spite of the hardships they faced. The second woman described how she enjoyed her adult years by socializing with many friends, despite her physical disability and broken engagement. After 50 years, she found her former fiance again later in life, and they lived together until his recent disability.

Perceptions of Being Married

With only one exception, the widows did not regret getting married. Most of the women could not imagine living any other way. Thinking back over their lives, 11 women noted that they had had "happy marriages" in spite of the ups and downs. They said that they expected that problems would occur, and they were grateful for the happy times they shared with their husbands. The remaining 3 women noted that at least their marriages produced children for whom they were grateful. For all 15 widows, marriage and motherhood were part of the same experience. They expected to marry, and having children was an integral part of marriage:

> Yeah, everyone has ups and downs. And I don't care how perfect a marriage is, there are certain times that you're going to argue, you're going to say things that you didn't mean. You can't help that, just living with someone, constantly, day in and day out, you're going to have arguments. I don't think that anyone can say that they haven't had ar-

guments. I don't care how good a marriage they've had. If they do, they're lying.

That is the way life has always been for me. I came from a family of 5, and my father came from a family of 13, and my mother 9, so, I just can't imagine life without a family.

Well, our life was fuller, home was more exciting. It wasn't like an everyday routine. When you have a baby in the home, why, there's an awful lot of changes. With all these things happening, why, now it makes me have a fuller life. I can think about these things. If all these things hadn't happened, then I'd be sitting.

I have had the companionship of my husband and of a family. I don't think that is something that can be replaced, regardless of what a person has. Really caring for each other.

All the widows seemed puzzled by the questions asking them to compare their lives to those of never-married women. Their first response was "I don't know anybody like that." After further probing, their responses were typical of the following:

I don't know of anyone. Not anyone close that I could voice an opinion about it. My husband's cousins, there's three of them that never married, but I don't know what they do. They live together, they're three old maids. The ugly sisters, what did he call them? They weren't good looking, they were ugly. I don't know too much about them. All I know is that they were disagreeable. They weren't pleasant to be around. I don't know of anything.

Well, I think that it all depends. If you have a great deal of love in your heart you will want children sooner or later. But, on the other hand, I suppose there are a lot of people in this world that would rather do other things. Like travel or I don't know, maybe a gorgeous home or spend money on other things. I myself would rather spend money on children.

I would not have been happy if I did not have children. I really feel sorry for people who don't. Now, you take people in this place, there are some of them who have never been married, and there are some who married late in life, and they have no one. I think that is a tragedy. Because the one thing that I have is my family, even if they are scattered all over the country, they are all good people, and they have all taken good care of their families, and they have all done reasonably well, and I can be proud of them. And I love them dearly.

I think they are more involved in dancing or something like that. If you never got married, you have to find an outlet of some kind. Because where I had my children and everything, they had other activities to go to and stuff like that.

Just as some of the never-married women had unrealistic views about the life of a married mother, the widows held stereotypic perceptions about women who did not marry or bear children. Curiously, all the women lived in senior citizen housing or were members of senior citizen groups, so they did know and live among women who were unmarried. Many of the widows also had siblings who never married or who did not bear children, but the status of never-married was peculiar to them.

The tension between marriage norms and actual life course experience was evident in their quotations. A woman was supposed to be a wife and a mother. All these women knew unmarried women, yet, they still perceived them as old maids or bereft of family. Even the never-married women knew what it was like to live with and care for others, including children, but several still romanticized how different their own family life could have been if given the chance. The alternative family subcareer they followed of helping maintain the autonomy of their family of orientation, though actually significant across these 15 lives, was still perceived as deviant in relation to the norm of marriage and motherhood.

SUMMARY

In old age, the women found themselves in similar circumstances. They described the present time as one of being alone, independent, and free from former responsibilities. They valued being independent in old age. Most were able to function independently because they had prepared themselves for this time by establishing a support system. For a second group of women, however, there was a current problem related to one of their life course careers, such as health or loss of a loved one, that signaled their vulnerability to future dependency. For a third group, there were several unresolved issues in their present circumstances that posed an even greater threat to their future.

Marital status was not a factor in differentiating women in terms of their perceptions about being alone. There were equal numbers in both groups of women in each of the above three categories, and most of the sample believed they had made a positive adjustment to old age. However, marital status did discriminate the sample in terms of their retrospective assessment of their lives. Most of the widows perceived that they had experienced all that life offered. More of the never-married expressed regrets about their lives or perceived that their lives were uneventful and dull. The widows had lived what they considered to be the acceptable lifestyle for women. They denied the reality of the never-married women's lives. The never-married women also had difficulty viewing their lives in perspective. They did not consider themselves as peculiar or as different as the widows did. Yet, they did not characterize their lives and contributions to their families with the enthusiasm the widows reserved for their description of themselves. Thus, the normative aspect of the auxiliary pathway of family keeper was hidden even to the women who lived it.

8

The Family Careers of Lifelong Single Women in Context

SINGLEHOOD AND FAMILY SURVIVAL

For women born in 1910, the family exerted considerable pressure on their life course decisions. The cultural norm for American women was to marry and reproduce, and families socialized their daughters to fulfill these expectations. Nearly 94% of women in this cohort eventually wed, attesting to the almost compulsory nature of marriage for women in the 20th century (Glick, 1977). But what of the more than 6% who did not? Typically, they are treated as deviants, or they are omitted from studies of the female life course (Uhlenberg, 1974).

The data presented here, which are consistent with the historical literature on singlehood, reveal that the proportion of women who remain single is a significant minority. Singlehood was discovered as a hidden alternative to the cultural ideology of marriage and motherhood. Rather than being deviants, the single women in this study fulfilled a related set of expectations for some members of their cohort and class. This alternative strategy is rooted in the Western European marriage pattern (Dixon, 1978; Watkins, 1984) associated with a stem family structure, where marriage strategies are tied to inheritance patterns and the economic conditions of the family and society (Berkner, 1973).

These never-married women followed a life course pathway that was consistent with older familistic norms of keeping a daughter at home to care for a widowed mother or aging parent (Hareven, 1977;

Laslett, 1972; Watkins, 1984). The familistic ideology promoted the use of various marriage strategies to ensure family survival, continuity, and control (Bourdieu, 1976; Watkins, 1984). To use an economic analogy (Acker, 1988; Rapp, 1982), families sent out some members to marry, reproduce, and extend the kin group, and kept others at home to maintain the original family. These family decisions were tied to cultural norms, demographic realities, economic conditions, and historical context.

Remaining single, then, was a normative process, marked by family subcareers. Family survival was promoted through the interdependence of women and their kin. The women revealed a mutual relationship with their families, and their experience of singlehood was correlated with a familistic ideology and marriage strategies rather than an independent choice to remain unattached. Today, the increasing incidence of singlehood among middle-class women is explained by their economic independence (Adams, 1972; Baker, 1968; Braito & Anderson, 1983). Also, historical studies show a variety of contexts in the past where significant groups of economically independent women chose a single life and formed communities of women apart from traditional family responsibilities (Chambers-Schiller, 1984; Freeman & Klaus, 1984; Hufton, 1984; Vicinus, 1985; Watkins, 1984). Certainly, these studies suggest the operation of individual choice, but for the most part, working-class women had fewer economic resources to support such independent decisions (Scott & Tilly, 1975). They were socialized to focus their life course decisions about work and intimate relationships around the survival needs of their families.

INTEGRATING LIFELONG SINGLE WOMEN AND FAMILY DEVELOPMENT

The discovery of the family-keeping roles of never-married women extends our understanding of family development across the life course by integrating their experiences into existing knowledge of working-class women and families. This integration is attempted through three levels of generality suggested by Runyan (1984): what is true of all women in the study, what is true for the two marital groups, and what is unique to individuals.

The Interdependence of Women and Their Families

At the general level, all the women in this study were connected to their families. The family was the focal point in their lives, the hub around which other life course careers were organized and described. They shared the familistic ideology, the experience of marginality, and the expectation of hard work from their socialization as daughters of working-class families. They shared the experience of coordinating their own life course decisions with the survival needs of their families. They had at least one intimate connection to another adult member of their family (i.e., parents, husbands, children, siblings). They were in similar circumstances in old age. Never-married women outlived their lifelong companions (i.e., mothers) just as widows outlived their husbands. They shared the experience, with the exception of one never-married woman, of caring for children in some variation of a mothering role. In caring for others throughout their lives, they had someone to care for or about them in old age. As the women aged, they experienced many of the same events. With the exception of one never-married woman, they all lost their parents. With the exception of a never-married woman and a widow, they all worked outside the home for some portion of their adult lives.

As members of a marginal class in industrial society, they were disadvantaged by class and gender. The "caring work" they provided was invisible—unpaid and devalued. Discussions of the invisible labor of women have focused on the activities of married women in housework, childcare, and parent care (Brody, 1985; Oakley, 1985; Rapp, 1982; Rubin, 1983), but in this study, the work of lifelong single women as family keepers was discovered as part of women's work in the family. The hidden dimensions of their family subcareers can be interpreted as part of the overall pattern of invisible, unpaid labor of women in keeping their families together.

The issues associated with independence, dependence, and interdependence are complex, and their use in this study is certainly not unique. The concept of interdependence is used to describe a variety of phenomena. For example, Crosby (1985) suggested the concept of interdependence to describe healthy marital relationships. Johnson (1977) used it to explain Japanese-American kinship relations. Fischer (1981) described how interdependence characterized the transitions in the mother-daughter relationship. Hareven's (1982b) study of French Canadian immigrants in New Hampshire revealed the interdependence of kin in maintaining the autonomy of the family under adverse economic conditions. Walker, Thompson, and Morgan (1987) assessed various indicators of interdependence, such as emotional attachment, in studying mother-daughter pairs. In this study, interdependence was associated with the lifelong caregiving roles of widowed and never-married women from the same birth cohort.

Family Keeping and Family Extension

At the group level, marital status differentiated their lives by focusing their caregiving on two distinct but interrelated processes of family extension and family maintenance. Widows extended their families by marrying and reproducing. They focused on husbands, children, and grandchildren. Never-married women fulfilled an auxiliary role of family maintenance. Its dimensions were caring for parents, being a lifelong companion, and serving as surrogate mother to siblings' children. Thus, the family life course consists of many subcareers (Feldman & Feldman, 1975), several of which are not tied to earlier biases of marital and parental status found in the family life cycle concept (see also Berkner, 1973; Elder, 1977; Hareven, 1987; Trost, 1977). The adult child/aging parent subcareer in this study was one of never-married women's lifelong family-keeping roles, but, in most of the parent caregiving literature, this role is reported to be done by middle aged married daughters (see also Brody, 1985; Finch & Groves, 1983; Troll, 1986). The evidence from the present study offers support for Brody's (1985) conceptualization of parent caring as a life course career, but is also a reminder of the hidden work of never-married women.

The never-married women and the widows also differed in their residential careers. Most of the never-married women lived with their parents for a good portion of their lives. Since they cared for their parents, they had the opportunity to work out their dependency in the parent-child relationship and resolve issues rooted in the family of orientation. The never-married women talked about a process of differentiation from their parents where they became independent from their parents' domination, but that did not occur, typically, until middle to later adulthood. The give and take in the parent-child relationship in the never-married women's experience was akin to the marital relationship the widows had with their husbands. Health was not a distinguishing factor during adulthood, but, in childhood, the never-married women were more likely to cite health reasons for delaying their transition to adulthood.

Individual Variation

Each woman had a unique history which can be interpreted as how she dealt with the constraints of working-class life. Correlated with permanent singlehood for this cohort was the strategy of keeping a younger daughter at home as lifelong companion and caregiver to aging parents. Although women have identified with their families historically, they have also been oppressed by them, as studies of working-class women have shown (see also Bott, 1971; Ferree, 1984; Rubin, 1976; Smith & Valenze, 1988). The never-married women in this study who felt they had the "best of both worlds" by remaining unwed but still having ties to children expressed this contradiction between individual and family needs. They resisted being devalued in marriage, but they also disassociated themselves from the devalued stereotype of old maid, a finding consistent with Hufton's (1984) studies of single women in 18th century England and France and Vicinus' (1985) study of 19th century teachers and reformers in America and England.

THE PERSISTENCE OF A DEVALUED STATUS

The use of the life course perspective allowed the interdependence of women and their families to be seen as a lifelong process. The qualitative life history interviews allowed the women to reveal their perceptions about themselves. Although their particular event histories differed, the women revealed a process of lifelong caregiving, regardless of marital status. The process of caregiving linked them with the development of their families. Their perceptions about the events and transitions in their life course careers challenge the stereotype of the old maid as bereft of family and allow the hidden subcareers in the family life course to emerge.

There was a discrepancy between the family roles women performed, which were accompanied by a sense of satisfaction and value, and their perception about the normative status of never-married women. The family keeper role of never-married women was essential and valued. They performed pivotal roles in maintaining their families of orientation. As caregivers to aging parents and surrogate mothers to siblings' children, they provided support and service. Widows extended their family roles to descending generations as they became mothers, grandmothers, and great-grandmothers. Never-married women's extensions were multidimensional—to ancestors; to parents, aunts and uncles; to lateral kin; and to the descendants of siblings (Allen & Pickett, 1987).

There was considerable evidence in this study, however, that the status of being never-married was not valued. Three findings suggest the devaluation of never-married status. First, the widows did not perceive similarities between their lives and never-married women's lives. They viewed them in stereotypic terms as old maids. They would not want to be a never-married woman. Second, 5 widows described how they almost became "old maids," but were saved from this fate by a late marriage. Third, never-married women who felt they led full and eventful lives thought they were different from other permanent singles. They did not perceive themselves as old maids. While few never-married women labeled themselves as such, 7 perceived they led dull, uneventful lives, but they did not perceive themselves as old maids. Thus, they did not identify with this devalued status; along with the widows, they believed that to be an old maid was to be deviant. The multiple family roles performed by never-married women over their lives were active and essential. They kept people alive, they provided relief from day-to-day responsibilities of married siblings, and they performed the symbolic function of keeping the past alive. Yet, the stereotype of the old maid persisted. They were aware of the status difference in being married versus being never-married, and the unmarried women appeared to compensate for it by disassociating themselves from the devalued status. Their lives, overall, gave testimony to the power of the family in socializing and preparing people for adult roles. Marriage and motherhood were the normative family roles for adult women in this context, but these roles were supported by the auxiliary family-keeping role reserved for never-married women. For all the women in this study, these roles served the goal of family survival and continuity.

Taking care of families describes the essence of the life course of women in this sample who were born in 1910. In their recollections, they described realistically the complex emotions associated with caring for families: the missed opportunities, the bitterness and disappointment, the heartbreak of separation and loss, and the rewards associated with intimate attachments over their life course.

SUMMARY

This study, guided by the life course perspective, examined the family careers of lifelong single women in relation to their widowed peers. Marital and parental subcareers differentiated women in adulthood, but all women in the sample were interdependent with their families through women's historic caregiving roles. The perspective offered here freed women's life course development from its traditional context; the wider context of family life course subcareers revealed how individual and family time were intertwined. An edited life history approach was used to examine the variation in women's experiences. The small sample and the singular cohort limit applying the results to other groups. However, the findings in this study were linked to the historically essential role of spinster found in the past.

Future investigations are needed to elaborate the family-keeping roles of childless, unmarried women. In particular, the parent-caring role, currently seen as the domain of middle aged, married daughters, was a lifelong process for single women in this study. Also, a study on the type of care never-married women receive from their fictive children might unravel the threat of isolation among elderly single women. Finally, the historical finding of communities of old women apart from traditional family arrangements warrants investigation in the present context. This study provided evidence of family connection, gleaned retrospectively. A fruitful comparison would be to examine the plans of young and middle aged single women for the communities they hope to establish in old age.

Appendix

DATA COLLECTION AND ANALYSIS FORMS

Initial Contact Interview

I am doing a study of women's lives who were born around 1910. I would like to begin by asking you a few questions about your life today:

1. What club/center(s) do you belong to?
2. Do you attend often?
3. What activities do you do?
4. How long have you been coming?
5. Do you live close by?
6. Where?
7. What type of work did you do? (occupation)
8. Did anyone else ever support you financially?
9. What was his/her occupation?
10. How far did you go in school?
11. Where were you born?
12. When?
13. When did you come to Syracuse?
14. Have you ever been married?
15. Current marital status:
16. How did your marriage(s) end?
17. When? (date/age)
18. Have you ever had children? (number)
19. What are their ages?
20. What is your religion?
21. Mother's and father's ethnicity:

Eligibility Status and Summary of Initial Contact:

Life Events Guide

List the major events that have happened in your life, starting with the present time and working back.

1980s

1970s

1960s

1950s

1940s

1930s

1920s

1910s

In-Depth Interview Guide

General Questions About Daily Activities:

To begin, let's talk about your life now.
How do you usually spend your time?
What do you do on a typical day?
How are these activities different from your life in the past?
How are they the same?

Importance of Family/Friends in One's Life:

Tell me about your family.
Tell me about your friends.
So far, you have mentioned————(list the people for her). As you think
    about others in your life, is there anyone else you would add?
Tell me about the most important person in your life today.
Tell me about the most important person in your life overall.

Life Events Guide:

Tell me about your "Life Events Guide." (After key events, probe with
    "how was your life different after that event?")
What was the high point in your life?
What was the low point in your life?
What other events have occurred that we haven't listed yet?
Tell me about yourself 10 years from now.

Perception of One's Life Events as Normative or Variant:

In what ways are the events that have happened to you the usual ones
    most people experience?
Some people think it makes a difference in your life if you marry and
    have children, and some people think it doesn't make that much
    difference at all. What do you think?

Never-Married Women:

Have you ever thought about what your life would have been like if you
    had married and had children? Tell me about it.
As you look back over your life, in what ways has it been similar to
    the lives of other women you know who have remained single
    like yourself?
In what ways has it been different?
In what ways has it been similar to the lives of women you know who
    married and had children?
In what ways has it been different?

Widows:

Have you ever thought about what your life would have been like if you
    had not married and did not have children? Tell me about it.
As you look back over your life, in what ways has it been similar to the
    lives of other women you know who married, had children, and
    are now widows?

In what ways has it been different?
In what ways has it been similar to the lives of women you know who
     did not marry?
In what ways has it been different?

Perception of Life Phases:

Some people say life is divided into phases, and others say, no, it's all
     the same. What do you think?
Is there a shape to your life?

Summary Statements:

Now that we have talked about some of the major parts of your life, I
     just have a few more questions. Are there any other events you
     have thought of as we've talked that you would like to add?
Some people say they have certain words (probe: sayings, proverbs) they
     live by. Does this apply to you? Do you have certain words or
     ideas you have come to live by?

Life History Information

Occupational History: For each job, request the following data:

1. Name of organization
2. Job title
3. Job duties
4. Full or part time
5. Dates worked
6. Reasons for leaving

Residential History: For each residence, request the following data:

1. Address
2. Who else lived there
3. Own or rent
4. Length of residence: moved in; moved out
5. Reason for moving
6. Comments

Health History:

1. How is your health?
2. Some people don't feel as well when they get older, and others feel about the same or better. How do you feel?
3. What major operations or illnesses have you had? Request dates and circumstances.

Family of Orientation:

1. Data about parents' marriage:
   A. Date of marriage, length, how did it end, when?
   B. Tell me about your parents' marriage:
2. Data about your mother and your father:
   A. Date of birth, birthplace, date of death, occupation, education.
   B. Tell me about your relationship with your mother; your father:
   C. Did anyone else serve as a "mother" or a "father" to you?
   D. Number of mother's brothers and sisters; of father's:
   E. Tell me about your relationship with each of their relatives: (their mother, father, sisters, brothers, others).
3. iblings: For each sibling, request the following:
   A. Gender; dates of birth, marriage, death; current marital status;occupation; number, sex, and age of children and grandchildren.
   B. Tell me about your relationship with each sibling and his/her children and grandchildren.

Widow's Family of Procreation:

1. Data about husband:
   A. Year of birth, birthplace, year of death, ethnicity, education, occupation, retirement date, causes and circumstances of death.
   B. Tell me about your husband:
2. Data about each of your children:
   A. Dates of birth, marriage, death; current marital status, occupation; number, sex, and age of your descendants.
   B. Tell me about your relationship with each of your descendants.

Coding Categories

100 Cohort Experiences

101   immigrants

102   women's work
103   the orphanage
104   historical events and their impact
105   other cohort experiences

200   Being Married and Not Being Married

206   the process of getting married
207   the process of not getting married
208   male/female relationships
209   the process of ending male/female relationships
210   perspectives on second marriages

300   Caretaking Roles and Relationships

311   relationships with parents and old people
312   relationships with children and younger people
313   relationships with siblings, peers, and friends
314   pets

400   The Darker Side of Family Life

415   deaths
416   divorce, separations, severed ties
417   physical and mental illness
418   abuse, violence, drunkenness
419   other family problems (in-laws, premarital pregnancy, etc.)

500   My Work Events and Perspectives on Work

520   education and training
521   being a "working girl"
522   separate and unequal: experiences with discrimination
523   how I view my work
524   retirement

600   Other Individual Life Course Events

625   women's bodily functions
626   my illnesses, diseases, operations, accidents, near death experiences
627   residential events
628   travel
629   driving a car

700 *Growing Old: My Life Today*

730 the woman's home and environment (dolls!)
731 daily routines (housekeeping, etc.)
732 perspectives about senior citizens
733 the most important person in my life today
734 perspectives about being alone

800 *Views of N-M and Widows About Themselves and Each Other*

835 never-married women view themselves
836 never-married women view widows
837 widows view themselves
838 widows view never-married women

900 *Life Review Processes: Defining My Past, Present, and Future*

939 high points and achievements
940 low points and tragedies
941 perceptions about what DIDN'T happen, regrets, disappointments,
relief, resignation, "you never miss what you never had",
reinterpreting events, etc.
942 perceptions about how change occurs
943 changes in my life
944 the type of life I have led (full, dull, hard, ordinary, etc.)
945 phases of my life
946 what I believe in (God, words of wisdom, prayer, ESP, etc.)
947 the most important person in my life overall
948 perspectives on the future; 10 years from now
949 my legacy: my purpose in life and what I will pass on

1000 *Methods Codes*

1050 perceptions of being interviewed
1051 observer comments
1052 inconsistencies in the data

References

Abrams, R. M. (1973). Reform and uncertainty: America enters the twentieth century: 1900-1918. In W. E. Leuchtenburg (Ed.), *The unfinished century: America since 1900*. Boston: Little, Brown.

Acker, J. (1988). Class, gender, and the relations of distribution. *Signs: Journal of Women in Culture and Society, 13*, 473-497.

Acker, J., Barry, K., & Esseveld, J. (1981). Feminism, female friends, and the reconstruction of intimacy. In H. Lopata & D. Maines (Eds.), *Research in the interweave of social roles: Vol. 2. Friendship* (pp. 75-108). Greenwich, CT: JAI.

Adams, M. (1972). The single woman in today's society: A reappraisal. In H. Wortis & C. Rabinowitz (Eds.), *The women's movement: Social and psychological lifestyles* (pp. 89-101). New York: AMS Press.

Adams, M. (1976). *Single blessedness*. New York: Basic Books.

Aldous, J. (1978). *Family careers: Developmental change in families*. New York: John Wiley.

Allen, K. R., & Pickett, R. S. (1987). Forgotten streams in the family life course: Utilization of qualitative retrospective interviews in the analysis of lifelong single women's family careers. *Journal of Marriage and the Family, 49*, 517-526.

Andersen, M. L. (1988). *Thinking about women: Sociological perspectives on sex and gender* (2nd. ed.). New York: Macmillian.

Baker, L. G. (1968). The personal and social adjustment of the never-married woman. *Journal of Marriage and the Family, 30*, 473-479.

Bell, R. R. (1981). *Worlds of friendship*. Beverly Hills, CA: Sage.

Berkner, L. K. (1973). The stem family and the developmental cycle of the peasant household: An 18th century Austrian example. In M. Gordon (Ed.), *The American family in social-historical perspective* (pp. 34-58). New York: St. Martin's.

Bernard, J. (1972). *The future of marriage*. New York: Bantam.

Bernard, J. (1981a). *The female world*. New York: Free Press.

Bernard, J. (1981b). The good provider role: Its rise and fall. *American Psychologist, 36*, 1-12.

Bertaux, D. (Ed.). (1981). *Biography and society: The life history approach in the social sciences*. Beverly Hills, CA: Sage.

Bertaux, D., & Bertaux-Wiame, I. (1981). Life stories in the bakers' trade. In D. Bertaux (Ed.), *Biography and society* (pp. 169-189). Beverly Hills, CA: Sage.

Bogdan, R., & Biklen, S. K. (1982). *Qualitative research for education*. Boston: Allyn & Bacon.

Boris, E., & Bardaglio, P. (1987). Gender, race, and class: The impact of the state on the family and the economy, 1790-1945. In N. Gerstel & H. E. Gross (Eds.), *Families and work* (pp. 132-151). Philadelphia: Temple University Press.

Bott, E. (1971). *Family and social network* (2nd ed.). New York: Free Press.

Bourdieu, P. (1976). Marriage strategies as strategies of social reproduction. In R.

Forster & O. Ranum (Eds. and Trans.), *Family and society* (pp. 117-144). Baltimore: Johns Hopkins University Press.

Braito, R., & Anderson, D. (1983). The ever-single elderly woman. In E. W. Markson (Ed.), *Older women: Issues and prospects* (pp. 195-219). Lexington, MA: Lexington Books.

Brim, O. G., Jr., & Ryff, C. D. (1980). On the properties of life events. In P. B. Baltes & O. G. Brim, Jr. (Eds.), *Life-span development and behavior: Vol. 3* (pp. 368-388). New York: Academic Press.

Brody, E. M. (1985). Parent care as a normative family stress. *The Gerontologist,* *25,* 19-29.

Brown, C. V. (1982). Home production for use in a market economy. In B. Thorne & M. Yalom (Eds.), *Rethinking the family: Some feminist questions* (pp. 151-167). New York: Longman.

Butler, R. N. (1968). The life review: An interpretation of reminiscence in the aged. In B. L. Neugarten (Ed.), *Middle age and aging* (pp. 486-496). Chicago: University of Chicago Press.

Carter, H., & Glick, P. C. (1976). *Marriage and divorce: A social and economic study.* Cambridge, MA: Harvard University Press.

Chambers-Schiller, L. V. (1984). *Liberty, a better husband: Single women in America: The generations of 1780-1840.* New Haven, CT: Yale University Press.

Chodorow, N., & Contratto, S. (1982). The fantasy of the perfect mother. In B. Thorne & M. Yalom (Eds.), *Rethinking the family: Some feminist questions* (pp. 54-75). New York: Longman.

Chudacoff, H. P. (1980). The life course of women: Age and age consciousness, 1865-1915. *Journal of Family History, 5,* 274-292.

Chudacoff, H. P., & Hareven, T. K. (1979). From the empty nest to family dissolution: Life course transitions into old age. *Journal of Family History, 4,* 69-83.

Collins, R. (1988). Women and men in the class structure. *Journal of Family Issues, 9,* 27-50.

Cornell, L. L. (1984). Why are there no spinsters in Japan? *Journal of Family History, 9,* 326-339.

Crosby, J. F. (1985). *Illusion and disillusion: The self in love and marriage* (3rd ed.). Belmont, CA: Wadsworth.

Cuber, J. F., & Harroff, P. B. (1965). *The significant Americans.* New York: Appleton-Century.

Dabrowski, I. (1983). Developmental job patterns of working-class women. *Qualitative Sociology, 6,* 29-50.

Davidoff, L. (1983). Class and gender in Victorian England. In J. L. Newton, M. P. Ryan, & J. R. Walkowitz (Eds.), *Sex and class in women's history* (pp. 16-71). London: Routledge & Kegan Paul.

Denzin, N. K. (1978). *The research act* (2nd ed.). New York: McGraw-Hill.

Dixon, R. B. (1978). Late marriage and non-marriage as demographic responses: Are they similar? *Population Studies, 32,* 449-466.

Duvall, E. (1971). *Family development.* Philadelphia: J. B. Lippincott.

Elder, G. H., Jr. (1974). *Children of the Great Depression: Social change in life experience.* Chicago: University of Chicago Press.

Elder, G. H., Jr. (1977). Family history and the life course. *Journal of Family History*, *2*, 279-304.

Elder, G. H., Jr. (1981). History and the family: The discovery of complexity. *Journal of Marriage and the Family*, *43*, 489-519.

Elder, G. H., Jr., & Rockwell, R. C. (1976). Marital timing in women's life patterns. *Journal of Family History*, *1*, 34-53.

Erikson, E. H. (1963). *Childhood and society* (2nd ed.). New York: W. W. Norton.

Erikson, E. H. (1975). *Life history and the historical moment.* New York: W. W. Norton.

Feldman, H., & Feldman, M. (1975). The family life cycle: Some suggestions for recycling. *Journal of Marriage and the Family*, *37*, 277-284.

Ferree, M. M. (1984). The view from below: Women's employment and gender equality in working class families. In B. B. Hess & M. B. Sussman (Eds.), *Women and the family: Two decades of change* (pp. 57-75). New York: Haworth.

Finch, J., & Groves, D. (1983). Introduction. In J. Finch & D. Groves (Eds.), *A labour of love: Women, work and caring* (pp. 1-10). London: Routledge & Kegan Paul.

Fischer, L. R. (1981). Transitions in the mother-daughter relationship. *Journal of Marriage and the Family*, *43*, 613-622.

Freeman, R., & Klaus, P. (1984). Blessed or not: The new spinster in England and the United States in the late nineteenth and early twentieth centuries. *Journal of Family History*, *9*, 394-414.

Gilligan, C. (1982). *In a different voice: Psychological theory and women's development.* Cambridge, MA: Harvard University Press.

Glaser, B. G., & Strauss, A. L. (1967). *The discovery of grounded theory: Strategies for qualitative research.* New York: Aldine.

Glick, P. C. (1977). Updating the life cycle of the family. *Journal of Marriage and the Family*, *39*, 5-13.

Glick, P. C. (1979). The future marital status and living arrangements of the elderly. *The Gerontologist*, *19*, 301-309.

Goody, J. (1972). The evolution of the family. In P. Laslett & R. Wall (Eds.), *Household and family in past time* (pp. 103-124). Cambridge: Cambridge University Press.

Gordon, L. (1982). Why nineteenth-century feminists did not support "birth control" and twentieth-century feminists do: Feminism, reproduction, and the family. In B. Thorne & M. Yalom (Eds.), *Rethinking the family: Some feminist questions* (pp. 40-53). New York: Longman.

Gove, W. (1972). The relationship between sex roles, marital status, and mental illness. *Social Forces*, *51*, 34-44.

Gubrium, J. F. (1976). Being single in old age. In J. F. Gubrium (Ed.), *Time, roles, and self in old age* (pp. 179-195). New York: Human Sciences Press.

Hajnal, J. (1965). European marriage patterns in perspective. In D. V. Glass & D. E. C. Eversly (Eds.), *Population in history* (pp. 101-143). London: Edward Arnold.

Hareven, T. K. (1977). Family time and historical time. *Daedalus*, *106*, 57-70.

Hareven, T. K. (1978). The search for generational memory: Tribal rites in industrial society. *Daedalus*, *107*, 137-149.

Hareven, T. K. (1982a). The life course and aging in historical perspective. In T. K. Hareven & K. J. Adams (Eds.), *Aging and life course transitions* (pp. 1-26). New York: Guilford.

Hareven, T. K. (1982b). *Family time and industrial time.* Cambridge: Cambridge University Press.

Hareven, T. K. (1984). Themes in the historical development of the family. In R. D. Parke (Ed.), *Review of child development research: Vol. 7. The family* (pp. 137-178). Chicago: University of Chicago Press.

Hareven, T. K. (1987). Historical analysis of the family. In M. B. Sussman & S. K. Steinmetz (Eds.), *Handbook of marriage and the family* (pp. 37-57). New York: Plenum.

Hartmann, H. (1981). The family as the locus of gender, class, and political struggle: The example of housework. *Signs: Journal of Women in Culture and Society, 6,* 366-394.

Havens, E. M. (1973). Women, work, and wedlock: A note on female marital patterns in the United States. *American Journal of Sociology, 78,* 975-981.

Hill, R. (1970). *Family development in three generations.* Cambridge, MA: Schenkman.

Hill, R. (1986). Life cycle stages for types of single parent families: Of family development theory. *Family Relations, 35,* 19-29.

Hill, R., & Mattessich, P. (1979). Family development theory and life-span development. In P. B. Baltes & O. G. Brim, Jr. (Eds.), *Life-span development and behavior: Vol. 2* (pp. 161-204). New York: Academic Press.

Hill, R., & Rodgers, R. H. (1964). The developmental approach. In H. T. Christensen (Ed.), *Handbook of marriage and the family* (pp. 171-211). Chicago: Rand McNally.

Hood, J. C. (1986). The provider role: Its meaning and measurement. *Journal of Marriage and the Family, 48,* 349-359.

Huber, J. (1988). A theory of family, economy, and gender. *Journal of Family Issues, 9,* 9-26.

Hufton, O. (1984). Women without men: Widows and spinsters in Britain and France in the eighteenth century. *Journal of Family History, 9,* 355-376.

Hull, G. T., Scott, P. B., & Smith, B. (Eds.). (1982). *All the women are white, all the blacks are men, but some of us are brave: Black women's studies.* Old Westbury, NY: Feminist Press.

Jaggar, A. (1983). *Feminist politics and human nature.* Totowa, NJ: Rowman & Allanheld.

Job, E. M. (1983). Retrospective life span analysis: A method for studying extreme old age. *Journal of Gerontology, 38,* 369-374.

Johnson, C. L. (1977). Interdependence, reciprocity and indebtedness: An analysis of Japanese American kinship relations. *Journal of Marriage and the Family, 39,* 351-362.

Jones, J. (1985). *Labor of love, labor of sorrow: Black women, work and the family from slavery to the present.* New York: Basic Books.

Katz, M. B. (1975). *The people of Hamilton, Canada West: Family and class in a mid-nineteenth century city.* Cambridge, MA: Harvard University Press.

Katz, M. B. (1983). *Poverty and policy in American history.* New York: Academic Press.

Keating, N., & Jeffrey, B. (1983). Work careers of ever married and never married retired women. *The Gerontologist, 23,* 416-421.

Kessler-Harris, A. (1977). Organizing the unorganizable: Three Jewish women and their union. In M. Cantor & B. Laurie (Eds.), *Class, sex, and the woman worker* (pp. 144-165). Westport, CT: Greenwood Press.

Kessler-Harris, A. (1982). *Out to work: A history of wage-earning women in the United States*. New York: Oxford University Press.

Komarovsky, M. (1962). *Blue collar marriage*. New York: Random House.

Langman, L. (1987). Social stratification. In M. B. Sussman & S. K. Steinmetz (Eds.), *Handbook of marriage and the family* (pp. 211-49). New York: Plenum.

LaRossa, R. (1977). *Conflict and power in marriage: Expecting the first child*. Beverly Hills, CA: Sage.

LaRossa, R., Bennett, L. A., & Gelles, R. J. (1981). Ethical dilemmas in qualitative family research. *Journal of Marriage and the Family, 43*, 303-313.

Lasch, C. (1977). *Haven in a heartless world*. New York: Basic Books.

Laslett, P. (1972). Introduction: The history of the family. In P. Laslett & R. Wall (Eds.), *Household and family in past time* (pp. 1-89). Cambridge: Cambridge University Press.

Lee, G. R. (1987). Comparative perspectives. In M. B. Sussman & S. K. Steinmetz (Eds.), *Handbook of marriage and the family* (pp. 59-80). New York: Plenum.

Lopata, H. Z., & Steinhart, F. (1971). Work histories of American urban women. *The Gerontologist, 11*, 27-36.

Macklin, E. D. (1980). Nontraditional family forms: A decade of research. *Journal of Marriage and the Family, 42*, 905-922.

Mason, K. O., Vinovskis, M. A., & Hareven, T. K. (1978). Women's work and the life course in Essex County, Massachusetts, 1880. In T. K. Hareven (Ed.), *Transitions* (pp. 187-216). New York: Academic Press.

Mattessich, P., & Hill, R. (1987). Life cycle and family development. In M. B. Sussman & S. K. Steinmetz (Eds.), *Handbook of marriage and the family* (pp. 437-469). New York: Plenum.

Matthews, S. H. (1986). *Friendships through the life course: Oral biographies in old age*. Beverly Hills, CA: Sage.

McLaughlin, V. Y. (1971). Patterns of work and family organization: Buffalo's Italians. In T. K. Rabb & R. I. Rotberg (Eds.), *The family in history* (pp. 111-126). New York: Harper.

Milardo, R. M. (Ed.). (1988). *Families and social networks*. Newbury Park, CA: Sage.

Mills, C. W. (1959). *The sociological imagination*. London: Oxford University Press.

Mindel, C. H., & Habenstein, R. W. (Eds.). (1976). *Ethnic families in America: Patterns and variations*. New York: Elsevier.

Modell, J., & Hareven, T. K. (1973). Urbanization and the malleable household: An examination of boarding and lodging in American families. *Journal of Marriage and the Family, 35*, 467-478.

Neugarten, B. L., & Weinstein, K. K. (1964). The changing American grandparent. *Journal of Marriage and the Family, 26*, 199-204.

Nock, S. L. (1979). The family life cycle: Empirical or conceptual tool? *Journal of Marriage and the Family, 41*, 15-26.

Oakley, A. (1985). *The sociology of housework* (2nd. ed.). Oxford: Basil Blackwell.

O'Rand, A. M. (1982). Socioeconomic status and poverty. In D. J. Mangen & W. A. Peterson (Eds.), *Research instruments in social gerontology: Vol. 2. Social roles and social participation* (pp. 281-341). Minneapolis: University of Minnesota Press.

Piven, F. F. (1985). Women and the state: Ideology, power, and the welfare state. In A. S. Rossi (Ed.), *Gender and the life course* (pp. 265-287). New York: Aldine.

Rapp, R. (1982). Family and class in contemporary America: Notes toward an understanding of ideology. In B. Thorne & M. Yalom (Eds.), *Rethinking the family: Some feminist questions* (pp. 168-187). New York: Longman.

Reichardt, C. S., & Cook, T. D. (1979). Beyond qualitative versus quantitative methods. In T. D. Cook & C. S. Reichardt (Eds.), *Qualitative and quantitative methods in evaluation research* (pp. 7-32). Beverly Hills, CA: Sage.

Rich, A. (1980). Compulsory heterosexuality and lesbian existence. *Signs: Journal of Women in Culture and Society, 5,* 631-660.

Rodgers, R. H. (1973). *Family interaction and transaction: The developmental approach.* Englewood Cliffs, NJ: Prentice-Hall.

Rosenberg, C. E. (1975). Introduction: History and experience. In C. E. Rosenberg (Ed.), *The family in history* (pp. 1-11). Philadelphia: University of Pennsylvania Press.

Rossi, A. S. (1980). Life-span theories and women's lives. *Signs: Journal of Women in Culture and Society, 6,* 4-32.

Rubin, L. B. (1976). *Worlds of pain: Life in the working-class family.* New York: Basic Books.

Rubin, L. B. (1983). *Intimate strangers: Men and women together.* New York: Harper Colophon.

Ruddick, S. (1982). Maternal thinking. In B. Thorne & M. Yalom (Eds.), *Rethinking the family: Some feminist questions* (pp. 76-94). New York: Longman.

Runyan, W. M. (1984). *Life histories and psychobiography.* New York: Oxford University Press.

Ryan, J. (Ed.). (1973). *White ethnics: Their life in working class America.* Englewood Cliffs, NJ: Prentice-Hall.

Ryder, N. B. (1965). The cohort as a concept in the study of social change. *American Sociological Review, 30,* 843-861.

Schatzman, L., & Strauss, A. L. (1973). *Field research: Strategies for a natural sociology.* Englewood Cliffs, NJ: Prentice-Hall.

Scott, J. W., & Tilly, L. A. (1975). Women's work and the family in nineteenth-century Europe. *Comparative Studies in Society and History, 17,* 36-64.

Scott, M., & Lyman, S. (1968). Accounts. *American Sociological Review, 33,* 46-62.

Shanas, E. (1979). The family as a social support system in old age. *The Gerontologist, 19,* 169-174.

Smith, D. S. (1979). Life course, norms, and the family system of older Americans in 1900. *Journal of Family History, 4,* 285-298.

Smith, R. L., & Valenze, D. M. (1988). Mutuality and marginality: Liberal moral theory and working-class women in nineteenth-century England. *Signs: Journal of Women in Culture and Society, 13,* 277-298.

Smith-Rosenberg, C. (1975). The female world of love and ritual: Relations between women in nineteenth-century America. *Signs: Journal of Women in Culture and Society, 1,* 1-29.

Spanier, G. B., Lewis, R. A., & Cole, C. L. (1975). Marital adjustment over the family life cycle: The issue of curvilinearity. *Journal of Marriage and the Family, 37,* 263-275.

Spradley, J. P. (1979). *The ethnographic interview.* New York: Holt, Rinehart and Winston.

Stack, C. B. (1974). *All our kin: Strategies for survival in a Black community.* New York: Harper Colophon.

Stein, P. J. (1978). The lifestyles and life chances of the never-married. *Marriage and Family Review, 1,* 1-11.

Taylor, S. J., & Bogdan, R. (1984). *Introduction to qualitative research methods* (2nd ed.). New York: John Wiley.

Tentler, L. W. (1979). *Wage-earning women: Industrial work and family life in the United States, 1900-1930.* New York: Oxford University Press.

Thorne, B. (1982). Feminist rethinking of the family: An overview. In B. Thorne & M. Yalom (Eds.), *Rethinking the family: Some feminist questions* (pp. 1-24). New York: Longman.

Treas, J. (1977). Family support systems for the aged: Some social and demographic considerations. *The Gerontologist, 17,* 486-491.

Troll, L. E. (Ed.). (1986). *Family issues in current gerontology.* New York: Springer.

Trost, J. (1977). The family life cycle: A problematic concept. In J. Cuisenier (Ed.), *The family life cycle in European societies* (pp. 467-481). The Hague: Mouton.

Uhlenberg, P. (1974). Cohort variations in family life cycle experiences of U. S. females. *Journal of Marriage and the Family, 36,* 284-292.

Uhlenberg, P. (1980). Death and the family. *Journal of Family History, 5,* 313-320.

Uhlenberg, P. (1988). Aging and the societal significance of cohorts. In J. E. Birren & V. L. Bengtson (Eds.), *Emergent theories of aging* (pp. 405-425). New York: Springer.

Van Gennep, A. (1960). *The rites of passage* (M. B. Vizedom & G. L. Caffee, Trans.). Chicago: University of Chicago Press.

Vicinus, M. (1985). *Independent women: Work and community for single women, 1850-1920.* Chicago: University of Chicago Press.

Voydanoff, P. (1988). Women, work, and family: Bernard's perspective on the past, present, and future. *Psychology of Women Quarterly, 12,* 269-280.

Walker, A. (1983). Care for elderly people: A conflict between women and the state. In J. Finch & D. Groves (Eds.), *A labour of love: Women, work and caring* (pp. 106-128). London: Routledge & Kegan Paul.

Walker, A. J., Pratt, C. C., Shin H., & Jones, L. L. (1989). Why daughters care: Perspectives of mothers and daughters in a caregiving situation. In J. A. Mancini (Ed.), *Aging parents and adult children.* Lexington, MA: Lexington Books.

Walker, A. J., Thompson, L., & Morgan, C. S. (1987). Two generations of mothers and daughters: Role position and interdependence. *Psychology of Women Quarterly, 11,* 195-208.

Watkins, S. C. (1984). Spinsters. *Journal of Family History, 9,* 310-325.

Welter, B. (1966). The cult of true womanhood, 1820-1860. *American Quarterly, 18,* 151-174.

Wilkinson, D. (1987). Ethnicity. In M. B. Sussman & S. K. Steinmetz (Eds.), *Handbook of marriage and the family* (pp. 183-210). New York: Plenum.

Wright, F. (1983). Single carers: Employment, housework and caring. In J. Finch & D. Groves (Eds.), *A labour of love: Women, work and caring* (pp. 89-105). London: Routledge & Kegan Paul.

Young, M., & Willmott, P. (1957). *Family and kinship in East London.* Glencoe, IL: Free Press.

Zaretsky, E. (1982). The place of the family in the origins of the welfare state. In B.

Thorne & M. Yalom (Eds.), *Rethinking the family: Some feminist questions* (pp. 188-224). New York: Longman.

Zinn, M. B., Cannon, L. W., Higginbotham, E., & Dill, B. T. (1986). The costs of exclusionary practices in women's studies. *Signs: Journal of Women in Culture and Society, 11,* 290-303.

About the Author

KATHERINE R. ALLEN is Associate Professor of Family Studies at Texas Woman's University. She received her M.A. and Ph.D. in Child, Family, and Community Studies and a Certificate in Gerontology from Syracuse University. In 1984, she received the Student of the Year Award from the National Council on Family Relations. She completed her undergraduate studies at the University of Connecticut. Currently, she is involved in research on the caregiving careers of older single men and women.

NOTES

NOTES

NOTES